Cambridge Architecture: A Concise Guide offers a brief, illustrated introduction to the architecture of Cambridge, using selected examples of buildings from the middle ages to the present day as the basis for an investigation into architecture itself. The author describes the way in which buildings are composed and how they may in turn be 'read', and introduces a number of levels of interpretation to those who may be unfamiliar with looking at buildings. Issues of iconography, questions of ethics, and the ways in which architecture may mirror society or indicate significant changes of taste are all touched upon.

The examples chosen are treated chronologically, but with frequent cross-referencing. Each chapter contains a map, locating the examples discussed, and notes for further reading. The book is aimed at anyone interested in the history of architecture, and assumes no previous technical knowledge of the subject.

CAMBRIDGE ARCHITECTURE

Frontispiece: St Peter's Church

CAMBRIDGE ARCHITECTURE

A Concise Guide

NICHOLAS RAY

CAMBRIDGE
UNIVERSITY PRESS

Published by the Press Syndicate of the University of Cambridge
The Pitt Building, Trumpington Street, Cambridge CB2 1RP
40 West 20th Street, New York, NY 10011–4211, USA
10 Stamford Road, Oakleigh, Melbourne 3166, Australia

© Cambridge University Press 1994

First published 1994

Printed in Great Britain at the University Press, Cambridge

A catalogue record for this book is available from the British Library

Library of Congress cataloguing in publication data

ISBN 0 521 45222 8 hardback
ISBN 0 521 45855 2 paperback

To Sarah

Contents

List of illustrations	*page*	xii
List of maps		xiv
Acknowledgements		xv
1	INTRODUCTION	1
	Arrangement	1
	Ways of seeing	2
	The language of architecture	3
	Cambridge style	4
	Other guides and histories, and notes on further reading	5
2	CAMBRIDGE BEFORE THE UNIVERSITY (UP TO 1280)	6
	Origins	6
	Norman architecture	7
	The Normans in Cambridge	10
	St Bene't's Church	11
	The Round Church (Church of the Holy Sepulchre)	12
	St Peter's Church – the font	14
3	THE PATTERN OF THE COLLEGES (1280–1515)	17
	University and college	17
	The pattern of a college	20
	Gothic architecture	21
	Corpus Christi College Old Court	25
	Queens' College	27
	Trinity College	30
	Jesus College	33

Contents

4   THE ENGLISH RENAISSANCE IN CAMBRIDGE (1515–1663)   37

The classical language   37

The five orders   40

Classical architecture comes to Cambridge   42

King's College Chapel – the chancel stalls and screen   43

Gonville and Caius College Gate of Honour   45

Christ's College Fellows' Building   48

Clare College   51

5   SEVENTEENTH- AND EIGHTEENTH-CENTURY CLASSICISM (1663–1800)   54

Wren in Cambridge   54

The Palladian taste   58

Trinity College Library   60

St Catharine's College – principal court   62

King's College Fellows' Building   64

The Master's Lodge, Peterhouse   66

6   NINETEENTH-CENTURY REVIVALISM (1800–1875)   69

Scholarship and romance   69

Gothic principles   73

Downing College   75

The Old University Library   78

Pembroke College   80

All Saints', Jesus Lane   82

7   LATE NINETEENTH- AND EARLY TWENTIETH-CENTURY ECLECTICISM (1875–1939)   86

'Queen Anne' style   86

The Arts and Crafts and Edwin Lutyens   87

Newnham College   90

The Law School complex   92

Clare Memorial Court and the University Library   95

48 Storey's Way   97

8   POST-WAR BUILDINGS (1939–1970)   101

The language of Modernism   101

Modernism in Cambridge   104

Gonville and Caius College Harvey Court   106

The History Faculty   108

St John's College Cripps Building   111

Clare Hall   113

Contents

9   BUILDINGS SINCE 1970   117
Fitzwilliam Chapel   120
Crystallographic Data Centre   121

Glossary   125
Bibliography   128
Index of buildings and people   132
Index of topics   135

Illustrations

	St Peter's Church	*frontispiece*
1	The tower of St Bene't's Church	*page* 13
2	The interior of the Round Church	15
3	The Norman font at St Peter's Church	16
4	The plan of Queens' College	22–3
5	The north side of Corpus Christi College Old Court	27
6	Trinity Great Court: hall, fountain and chapel	31
7	Jesus College: Early English arches at the entrance to the chapter house of the former convent of St Radegund	35
8	The five orders, from Serlio's *L'Architettura*, First Book	41
9	The stalls and chancel screen in King's College Chapel	44
10	Gonville and Caius College Gate of Honour with the Old University Library beyond	46
11	Two plates from Serlio's *L'Architettura*, Fourth Book	47
12	Christ's College Fellows' Building	49
13	Clare College, view of the west range	53
14	Trinity College Library: section	61
15	St Catharine's College	63
16	King's College Fellows' Building	65
17	Detail of the staircase balustrade at the Master's Lodge, Peterhouse	67
18	Downing College: the Master's Lodge	77
19	The Old University Library, north-west corner	79
20	The Red Building, Pembroke College	81
21	All Saints', Jesus Lane	84
22	Newnham College	91
23	The Law School complex: part of the north façade	93

24 The University Library 97

25 The living room and dining room of 48 Storey's Way 99

26 Gonville and Caius College Harvey Court: section perspective and site plan 107

27 Main reading room of the History Faculty 109

28 St John's College Cripps Building 113

29 Clare Hall, the Family Walk 115

30 Fitzwilliam College Chapel 121

31 The Cambridge Crystallographic Data Centre 123

Maps

---

1 Map showing buildings referred to in chapter 2   *pages* 8–9

2 Map showing buildings referred to in chapter 3   18–19

3 Map showing buildings referred to in chapter 4   38–9

4 Map showing buildings referred to in chapter 5   56–7

5 Map showing buildings referred to in chapter 6   70–1

6 Map showing buildings referred to in chapter 7   88–9

7 Map showing buildings referred to in chapter 8   102–3

8 Map showing buildings referred to in chapter 9   118–9

Acknowledgements

1–3, 5–7, 9, 10, 12, 13, 15–25 and 27–31, photographs © James Austin, by permission of the Master and Fellows of Corpus Christi College, the Vicar of the Round Church, the Master and Fellows of Trinity College, the Master and Fellows of Jesus College, the Provost and Fellows of King's College, the Master and Fellows of Gonville and Caius College, the Master and Fellows of Christ's College, the Master and Fellows of Clare College, the Master and Fellows of St Catharine's College, the Master and Fellows of Peterhouse, the Master and Fellows of Downing College, the Principal and Fellows of Newnham College, the Bursar, Master and Fellows of Churchill College, the Secretary of the Faculty Board of History, the Master and Fellows of St John's College, the President and Fellows of Clare Hall, and the Master and Fellows of Fitzwilliam College.

The plan of Queens' College (4) is reproduced by permission of the Royal Commission on the Historical Monuments of England and the section through the Library of Trinity College (14) by permission of the Warden and Fellows of All Souls' College, Oxford. Drawings of Harvey Court (26) are reproduced by permission of Sir Leslie Martin, Colin St J. Wilson and Patrick Hodgkinson.

I am indebted to James Austin for his photographs and to a number of colleagues in the Cambridge Historic Buildings Group for suggestions and criticisms, in particular Anthony Baggs, Thomas Cocke and Deborah Howard. I have benefited from conversations and correspondence with E. F. Mills, Berenice Schreiner, Kevin Taylor and others. Naturally the responsibility for errors of fact and judgement must remain mine. I must also thank my family and members of my practice, who have been patient with the demands on my time that this book has entailed, and Penny Hatfield who did most of the word processing.

CHAPTER 1

Introduction

ARRANGEMENT

This book is designed so that it can be read in preparation for a visit to Cambridge, as an introduction to the buildings of the University and colleges. But it is also intended to contribute to an understanding of architecture more generally.

It is arranged chronologically. Each chapter contains some comments on the characteristics of the architecture of the period concerned before considering a number of examples in detail. These have usually been chosen for their intrinsic worth but some are included in order to give an idea of the variety of buildings which warrant attention. Each chapter is provided with a map which identifies the principal buildings discussed, so that the concise guide can also be used to plan an afternoon's visiting and to accompany the visitor in front of the buildings themselves. Technical terms have been used but these are usually introduced in the first part of each chapter and a glossary has been included at the back. There are frequent cross-references so that works elsewhere of the same period, or by the same architect, may be mentioned, or neighbouring buildings of a different period alluded to in order to make a comparison. Finally, at the end of each chapter are some notes for further reading. This guide is necessarily dependent upon the original research of others and on previous treatments of the same buildings in other guide books; the references are intended to serve as an acknowledgement of this debt. Full titles are given in the bibliography at the end of the book.

Most of what is described is readily visitable, though permission may have to be sought to see some of the interiors. Colleges often limit visits during the early summer, in the examination term. In his 1925 *Illustrated Guide to Cambridge* Frank Rutter reassured his readers that public access to the Cambridge courts was 'practically unrestricted in daytime, and the College servants will be found usually to be civil, obliging, and sometimes communicative'. These were words written before the huge increase in tourism: a phenomenon which has benefited all of us in that we have seen and experienced more places in the world than most of our forefathers were able to, but which has its obvious drawbacks. We are all tourists, but I hope this book will help to turn an appreciation of Cambridge and its buildings into something more than merely touristic.

There are many different ways of seeing Cambridge. It is possible to appreciate the buildings as compositions of mass and line and to enjoy the way in which their planes and surfaces catch the low East Anglian light. We can admire the way in which the architect has handled wall surface, observe the depth of the reveal within which the window has been placed, and note the smooth creamy texture of the stone and its contrast with the cobbled courtyard. Not only is the eye involved; we feel the texture of the fabric and are aware of the echo of our footfall.

Another level of our understanding (not necessarily more profound than the reverie that may be induced by a sensuous appreciation) can be reached by understanding where these materials come from and how they were put together – whether the stone is Ancaster or Clipsham or whether the brick is from nearby Burwell and was fired in the eighteenth or nineteenth century. We may also admire the compositional skill of the architect in the arrangement of the building on plan, something that is less easy to appreciate immediately from the vertical expression in façade: how has the pattern of staircase and room, of column frame and massive wall, been manipulated both to meet the needs of the patron and to affect us who use or visit the buildings? What was the contribution of the architect and how much did the condition of patronage determine what it was possible to build? How then does the building reflect, represent or even symbolise the social conditions within which it was conceived?

We will note the effect of the British climate on the placing of whole buildings, the weathering of materials and also the way in which even small-scale details have been fashioned in response to it. In some cases the financial constraints within which the schemes have been conceived will be obvious; in others we will never know the struggles that the designer encountered in reconciling conflicting claims of budget and brief. It would take many books this length to look at even the selected examples in all of these ways, so the way in which each building is discussed is necessarily partial. I hope that cumulatively an experience of analysing buildings may build up so that readers can remedy the many deficiencies for themselves.

One thing is certain: the way in which we ourselves understand buildings is inevitably conditioned by the society we live in, and by the history of the ways that these buildings and places have been seen in the past. 'The Backs' (the stretch of fields and gardens either side of the River Cam running behind St John's, Trinity, Trinity Hall, Clare, King's and Queens') may serve as an example. Until 1750 this area acted as the town drain and a commercial waterway for barges, and the college buildings turned their backs to it (this accounts for the different façade treatments in Wren's Trinity College Library, p. 60) though Loggan's 1688 plan shows a bowling green and lawn behind King's. By the time of the King's Fellows' Building (p. 64) Gibbs was happy to plan rooms symmetrically facing on to the court and out towards the Backs and Charles Bridgeman proposed a project for improvements, which was never carried out. In 1779 'Capability' Brown, perhaps Britain's most famous landscape architect, acting on behalf of St John's, drew up a scheme (also unexecuted) for treating the whole area as a unified park, and in 1831 Rickman and Hutchinson's New Court for the same college (p. 72) boldly fronted this landscape with its stone screen and arcade.

In this century Giles Gilbert Scott's University Library (p. 95) began the collegiate and university development of the other side of the river. The Backs were seen by Pevsner in 1970 as the 'campus of the future . . . a precinct much larger than the precincts of the individual colleges had been in the past, yet a precinct all the same'. Meanwhile twentieth-century film and television documentaries and dramas that are set in Cambridge invariably show a disproportionate footage of the Backs because they have become not only a central physical focus, but also a potent symbol of Cambridge. Though it is possible for us to construct the historical state of the Backs at any one period, it is inevitable that our understanding should be conditioned by how we have learnt to see it. It is the same with our reading of individual buildings and the messages they convey.

THE LANGUAGE OF ARCHITECTURE

In many instances in this book, especially when talking about classical architecture and when looking at façades, I shall use a linguistic analogy – architecture as a language. There are other analogies we could employ, of course, and each of them has its advantages. The gastronomic analogy is a common one: the architect has a number of ingredients out of which everything from an unwholesome *mélange* to a cordon bleu masterpiece can be concocted; we discriminate between the products by the exercise of taste – and so on. Both these analogies presuppose that the business of architecture is a self-conscious activity: buildings do not just turn out one way or another according to the circumstances and constraints we have touched upon, they are consciously conceived. At different periods of history those who conceive them may be technicians (masons or engineers), dilettantes (the Master of a college for example) or professionals (acting on behalf of clients for a fee), and very frequently combinations of all of these. It is because buildings are self-conscious artefacts that they can tell us something not only about the society which produced them, but also about the individuals who were principally responsible for their design. They can convey messages to us that the designer intended, often by the use of symbols which the viewer would be expected to understand, or by a whole system of symbols (an iconography). So at a number of levels we may expect to 'read' a building somewhat as one might read a text. This linguistic analogy (which is convenient but by no means comprehensive) incidentally has a longer pedigree than the fashionable 'structuralism' of the twentieth century, and can be traced back to French books of the mid-eighteenth century.

CAMBRIDGE STYLE

The architectural character of the city and University is therefore created by the assembly of individual buildings, many of which have been crafted by the designers and their patrons with purposes which transcend the merely utilitarian. Between these consciously crafted works, and acting in some sense as a foil, survive buildings whose aspirations are less elevated and which speak in a common tongue or vernacular. Often it is the conjunction of high art and the vernacular which gives a place its unique character. One example would be King's Parade where shops and houses of many different ages and styles lie opposite the neo-Gothic screen designed in 1823 by William Wilkins. Much of this book is necessarily concerned with this use of style (what do we mean by neo-Gothic, and what did Wilkins intend by it?) but stylistic description and analysis is used not as an end in itself, rather as a means for understanding the aims of the architect. Because style is the most obvious and easily describable of a building's attributes, it is often asserted that a change of style will improve the quality of the architecture, or even hasten an improvement in the society which produced it (see the description of Pugin's position on p. 73). Though this is demonstrably not the case, it is arguable that at any given period only a limited range of styles would appear to be available to the designer. An original architect makes acceptable for the first time, or very frequently rehabilitates and re-authenticates, a manner which was previously regarded as incapable of carrying appropriate meanings. These are the controversial buildings of their time. Meanwhile most architects are working within a manner (or paradigm) that has already been established where their skill, or otherwise, is evident in the way in which they handle the architectural language they have inherited. Examples of both types of architecture form the detailed studies in the chapters which follow.

Architecture is a complex art, intimately related to the social conditions within which it is created, and can therefore be as profitably studied at a theoretical level through the discipline of social anthropology as through aesthetics. But this book concentrates on the close examination of the architecture itself, in particular by paying attention to the way in which individual architects articulate the language they choose or are constrained to adopt. Buildings for the colleges in Cambridge are specially pertinent examples to study because, unusually, the way in which they are inhabited has changed so little over the centuries. In the nineteenth and early twentieth centuries the arguments for a new style of architecture were frequently based not only on the emergence of new technologies but also on the need to provide for uses which were unprecedented – the railway station for example, or the laboratory. Rooms for undergraduates on the other hand or the requirements of a college library in Cambridge have changed remarkably little. Central heating is considered normal and more bathrooms have been provided (often to meet the needs of conference delegates rather than students); the library catalogue may be on disk or microfiche but the space needs of students to read books in natural light with ready access to other volumes in a college collection are unchanged. The brief for a new college, such as Churchill of 1958 (p. 105) or Robinson College of 1974 (p. 106), has not altered fundamentally since the middle ages, though for a college to be built all at once is a relatively recent phenomenon. The survival of particular patterns of planning is therefore not merely conservatism and nostalgia, though these are powerful influences at certain times. An argument for a changed external expression in buildings within the same college may require subtler functional justifications (see the comparison between Christ's College Fellows' Building of 1640–3 and the adjacent nineteenth-century building by J. J. Stevenson on p. 50).

Other guides and histories, and notes on further reading

There are many guides to the buildings of Cambridge This concise guide is intended to be complementary to them. Some have numerous illustrations with captions describing the images and are arranged topographically. Others are histories of the University and mention buildings incidentally. This book borrows its title from John Willis Clark's volume, first published in 1898 and last reprinted in 1949, which took most of its material from the monumental *Architectural History of the University of Cambridge* (1886, reprinted by Cambridge University Press with a new introduction in 1988) which he had earlier written with his uncle, Robert Willis. As reference works the two-volume Royal Commission on Historical Monuments, *City of Cambridge* (1959) and the Victoria County History, *Cambridgeshire and the Isle of Ely* (1948) are invaluable, as is the indefatigable Nikolaus Pevsner's *Cambridgeshire* of 1970, part of the Buildings of England series. The most recent comprehensive survey is Tim Rawle's *Cambridge Architecture* (1984). An excellent walking guide is Kevin Taylor's *Central Cambridge*.

For an extended meditation on the 'pastness' of the past, see David Lowenthal's *The Past is a Foreign Country* and for a recent analysis of tourism as a sociological phenomenon John Urry's *The Tourist Gaze*.

For the analogy touched on here with the way certain historians have thought about how scientists work, and in particular the use of the term 'paradigm' as a framework within which 'normal' science (or in this case architecture) takes place, see Thomas Kuhn's *The Structure of Scientific Revolutions*.

CHAPTER 2

Cambridge before the University
(up to 1280)

ORIGINS

As its name implies, Cambridge has always been a significant crossing point on its river, where there was sufficient firm ground either side to allow a ford, a ferry and later a bridge. To the north the Fens, not drained or enclosed until the eighteenth century, were a continuous marshland almost as far as Lincoln. Cambridge lies on a diagonal swathe of level firmer ground, later to be the course of the Roman Icknield Way, from the Thames valley northeastwards towards the Brecklands and Norfolk. There is archaeological evidence for settlements in the late Bronze Age (1000–500 BC) and Iron Age (500 BC to the Roman occupation in AD 43). The Romans established a civil settlement on Castle Hill, just above the crossing point of the Cam on the site of the present Magdalene Bridge. The town wall went up Pound Hill and Mount Pleasant, encircling the present Shire Hall, and ran slightly north of Chesterton Lane about on the line of the southern façade of St Giles' Church. St Peter's (discussed below) contains Roman bricks which may have formed part of this wall. The settlement was bisected (roughly SE–NW) by the Via Devana, crossing Akeman Street north of the river; its route northwards is marked today by the long straight Huntingdon Road.

It is not certain what the Roman name for Cambridge was. But the name of the river above the town, the Granta, is the cause of the present name because Bede (c. 673–735) refers to 'Grantacaister', and in the Domesday Book of 1086 the town is called 'Grentebrige' and had 375 houses around the castle. Only in the late eleventh century do we find 'Cantebrige', and only when Cambridge got its present name were the lower reaches of the Granta named the Cam.

During the so-called dark ages Cambridge lay between the rival kingdoms of Mercia and East Anglia and archaeological evidence for the two settlements on either side of the river is furnished by cemeteries. Those on what is now St John's College playing fields, at Madingley Road, and at Newnham Croft have yielded grave goods dating back to the fifth century which indicate that the Mercian settlers were connected with Slesvig in Denmark, but may also have included surviving Romano-British elements. The newer arrivals, the Angles, left evidence of burials in the area of what was to become the medieval town: Jesus Lane, Sidney Street and Rose Crescent. Arthur Grey surmised that the river crossing had been destroyed and was only reconstructed by King Offa in the eighth century. A Viking invasion of 875 brought both townships under Danish control and the area around Bridge Street became the centre of the community and an important trading port. The dedication of the nearby church to St Clement (patron saint of Danish sailors) recalls this important period of the town's history. In 921 the Danes submitted to the Saxon King, Edward the Elder, but the Anglo-Danish town was destroyed by fire in 1010 as part of the last wave of Danish invasions. Presumably it was quickly rebuilt because the construction of St Bene't's Church (see below) had begun by 1025. Apart from churches, all the buildings have disappeared. They would have been timber framed, with wattle and daub, and thatch-roofed, or built of cob (mud reinforced with straw), a building technique that survived into the twentieth century in Devon.

NORMAN ARCHITECTURE

The 1066 Norman invasion brought with it not only a confident and effective people who established a lasting dynasty, but also a style of architecture, for both secular and religious buildings, of much greater sophistication than the primitive pre-conquest Saxon style.

Like Britain, Europe had been subject to violent political and social upheavals for several hundred years, but from the coronation of Charlemagne as Holy Roman Emperor in 800 AD sufficient stability had been maintained to allow the development of a massive round-arched architecture, where the most important volumes were vaulted. The principal ingredients of the monastic plan emerged during the same period: a church with a cloister on its south side with dormitory, refectory (or dining room), kitchen and ancillary rooms either attached or above the arcades; nearby would be a library, houses for the abbot, guest houses and hostels for pilgrims. Despite nearly two centuries of unrest following Charlemagne's death, the round-arched style became the basis of 'Romanesque' and the monastic plan was to appear in the important cultural centres of northern Europe, and be echoed in the arrangement of the Cambridge colleges. The Viking invaders who settled in Normandy had converted to Christianity and by the middle of the eleventh century, at Jumièges and St Etienne at Caen, had developed one of the most powerful versions of the Romanesque style. Norman buildings in England derive from these examples; indeed after 1066 all the most

Map 1

Ⓐ St Bene't's Church
Ⓑ Church of the Holy Sepulchre
   (The Round Church)
Ⓒ St Peter's Church

Other sites and buildings mentioned
① Castle Hill
② Barnwell Priory
   (St Mary Magdalene)
③ School of Pythagoras

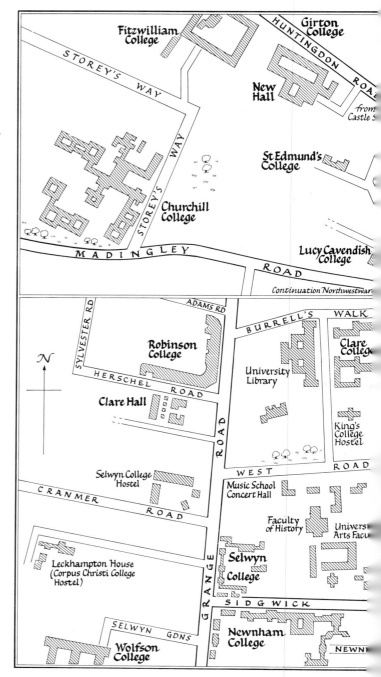

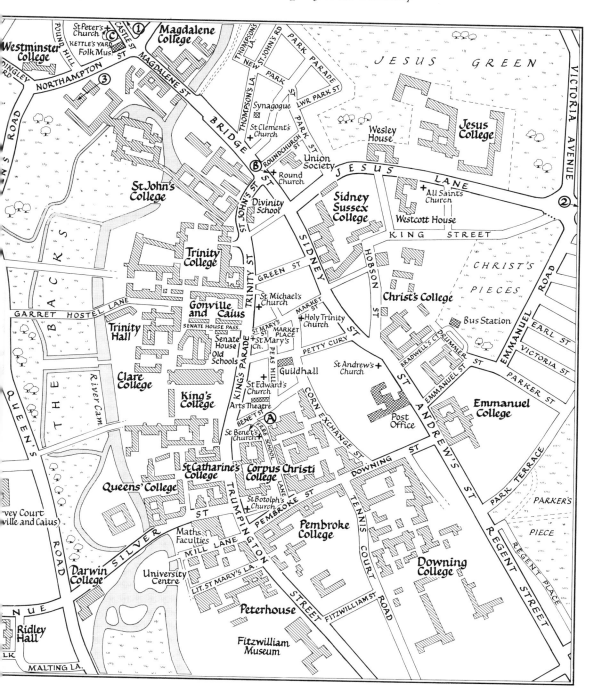

original and impressive Norman buildings are in England rather than in France, perhaps because William brought with him the most inventive and ambitious of his subjects. Durham, with its castle and cathedral at either end of an island citadel, is the clearest indication of the forceful character of its makers; the cathedral is perhaps the most imposing work of architecture of its date anywhere in Europe. The cathedral at Ely, some 20 miles north of Cambridge, begun in 1083 is almost as fine. Unlike Durham's, its nave is not vaulted, but the wall architecture is astonishingly complex and powerful. There are three levels: the arcade, a gallery and high-level windows or clerestories. All have round arches, or rather layers of arches. In the arcade and gallery these are held on stumpy blocks on cylindrical shafts attached to massive composite piers, or (in alternate bays) on the capitals of huge cylindrical columns. The surfaces are bare: only in places do the zig-zag mouldings characteristic of the Norman style appear, but in the middle ages all of the surfaces would have been painted. Ely was a Benedictine foundation, and fragments of the extensive monastery lie to the south of the cathedral and have been incorporated into buildings for the cathedral authorities and the King's School.

THE NORMANS IN CAMBRIDGE

In Cambridge, William the Conqueror's sheriff, Picot, destroyed twenty-seven houses on Castle Hill to create a stronghold in 1068. He was travelling south from York, and raised castles at Lincoln and Huntingdon *en route*. As the Royal Commission on Historical Monuments points out, 'what the Roman doubtless had in mind in Claudian times, the Norman achieved a thousand years later, and thus made possible the future prosperity of the borough'. Picot's castle had a mound or motte 13 m high, which remains today as an admirable point from which to survey the city. In 1092 Sheriff Picot established a priory on the site of the present St Giles'. Later, in 1112, it was moved to a site at Barnwell, some two miles east of Cambridge, and housed Augustinian Canons. About twenty years later there was a second religious foundation to the east of Cambridge, St Radegund's, though the church was not constructed there for another quarter century, on the site of what is now Jesus College (p. 33). Beyond Barnwell Priory the Leper Hospital was established, and nearby was Stourbridge Common, the site of a fair held every summer that was nationally important.

The diminutive chapel of St Mary Magdalene is all that remains of the Leper Hospital. Even though it is now set below the noisy dual carriageway leading out from Cambridge to Newmarket, as Rawle suggests, 'there is something about this modest little building that is very alluring'. Apart from early fifteenth-century re-roofing, a mid-nineteenth-century east window and the west windows installed by George Gilbert Scott during a restoration in 1867, very little has altered in eight and a half centuries. The massive flint walls and the south-facing windows and doors are untouched, and this authenticity perhaps contributes to its atmosphere. The zig-zag carvings noted at Ely can be seen over the chancel arch and externally over the tiny round-arched windows which have elaborately carved columns. There is evidence that the chancel originally had a quadripartite vault since some stumpy shafts appear. From within the simple barn-like nave the relative elaboration of the chancel arch forms an effective contrast with the rough rubble walls. Again, however, we must imagine these smoothly plastered and richly painted in the twelfth century.

So by the last quarter of the thirteenth century Cambridge had seventeen churches, eleven of which survive today, and nine religious houses or monastic foundations, but as yet no colleges nor any visible manifestation of a university.

An important domestic survival from the end of the twelfth or beginning of the thirteenth century is the so-called 'School of Pythagoras', now part of St John's College, but for nearly 700 years the property of Merton College, Oxford. Only about a dozen houses of this kind remain in England; all of them, including this, have been much altered. The house seems to have consisted of a rectangular hall raised on a vaulted stone undercroft with a short two-storey thirteenth-century wing, the upper floor of which acted as a separate sitting room or 'solar'. It is difficult to be sure whether any of the visible fabric is as old as we know the house to be because there have been so many re-facings and repairs. On the south-east side the tall buttresses are probably original; the doorway adjacent is about 1800. On the upper floor the paired window within the semicircular recess is on the original pattern though much repaired; the bay window and staircase are unfortunate additions of the 1960s.

ST BENE'T'S CHURCH

St Bene't's (or parts of it) is the oldest church in the city, and in the county of Cambridgeshire, and has the oldest visible fabric. The Victoria County History surmises that, because of the fragmentary nature of its parish, later parishes were carved out of it and it may therefore also be the earliest religious foundation in the southern part of Cambridgeshire. Much of the ancient fabric survived until a mid-nineteenth-century restoration but now only the tower (Fig. 1), the external angles of the nave and most of the south wall of the chancel are Saxon. The three tiers of the tower step back slightly as they rise, and are formed of uncoursed rubble with 'long and short' quoins at the corner, a simple but effective way of stabilising the building and forming a correct angle that is characteristic of Saxon work. The paired windows on the third stage facing north and west are original, as are all the circular openings. The four single-arched windows are insertions of 1586. The column in the twin openings is set centrally in the thick wall so that the arches seem to rest on a beam or bracket. The west windows below are fifteenth-century. (Because some of its motifs are continental in origin, a faint recollection of the classical language that was half-remembered in Charlemagne's empire and only fully revived in the Renaissance, it is necessary to use some terms that are not defined until chapter 4.) Inside, the tower archway is worth examining in detail. The semicircular arch and piers are absolutely plain, and have the same long and short slabs that reinforce the corners of the tower outside. Placed against the structural arch either side is a moulded surround which forms a rectangular and then a half-round attached pilaster and column, and which carries around over the archway. This is intersected at the springing of the arch by what looks like the cornice or entablature carrying across the wall face at either side and breaking forward over the pilasters. Instead of the frieze of this cornice receiving decoration, as one might expect, the semicircular arch moulding comes to rest on two carved monsters which sit on top of the entablature. Linguistically, it is as if the words in a sentence have been jumbled up, and the result is quite ungrammatical. But that is not to say that the meaning is unclear. Indeed there is something poignant about these Saxon masons celebrating the entry to their thick-walled tower by the application of decorative motifs, precedents for which in France and Germany they must somehow have been aware of. There is also something characteristically English in the graphic, or two-dimensional, way in which decoration has been applied to structure: a trait which is abundantly apparent in later 'Decorated' and 'Perpendicular' Gothic buildings (see p. 24).

THE ROUND CHURCH (CHURCH OF THE HOLY SEPULCHRE)

Despite almost complete rebuilding by Salvin in 1841, the Round Church remains the best building in Cambridge from which to gain a sense of Norman architecture (Fig. 2). The church owes its origin to the Abbot of Ramsey who granted money in about 1120 for the construction of a 'monasterium' in honour of God and the Holy Sepulchre. Circular-plan buildings to guard a tomb have Roman and early Christian antecedents, and round churches are frequently connected with orders which were founded to guard the Holy Sepulchre in Jerusalem: there were perhaps eleven altogether in England. Originally there would have been only the circular nave and a small semicircular apse. In the fifteenth century a chancel, north and south aisles, and a large polygonal belfry were added and larger windows inserted in the original circular walls. Salvin destroyed all that and returned the main part of the building to what he thought it would have been like in the twelfth century. The vaults in the nave were rebuilt, based on the archaeological evidence of the springers over the surviving circular columns. The whole of the aisle vaults were rebuilt at the same time, and new openings and alterations, including the addition of the bell turret, made to the fifteenth-century chancel.

All of this was done, nevertheless, with a thorough attempt at archaeological correctness, re-using in the nave the Norman material wherever possible (for a

1 The tower of St Bene't's Church

discussion of the philosophy of nineteenth-century restoration see pp. 73–4). We should not be prevented, by our knowledge of its history, from using this example to investigate and admire the space and structure of Norman architecture. Like Charlemagne's octagonal Palatine Chapel at Aachen at the end of the eighth century, the ring of vaults held on massive masonry is weighty, solid and reassuring, while at the same time, because of the circular plan and the changing diagonal views that that permits, spatially complex and subtle. This is monumental architecture of a high order, where the rhythm of pierced openings is enhanced by the addition of decoration at selected points – the springing of the arches and the capitals. The graphic two-dimensional character of the arch at St Bene't's had been superseded by an integrated system of column, wall and window opening which moulds the space of the interior in a powerful and convincing way.

ST PETER'S CHURCH – THE FONT

One other example will serve to illustrate Norman building in Cambridge, a 'fitting' rather than a whole building, the font in the tiny church of St Peter's on Castle Street (Fig. 3). It is the surviving remnant of a twelfth-century building consisting of a nave, chancel, south aisle, west tower and spire. By the mid-eighteenth century the church had ceased to be used and had fallen into decay. Since the parish had been united with St Giles' in 1650, it was rebuilt in its reduced form in 1781 re-using much of the existing material, which includes the Roman bricks mentioned earlier, the twelfth-century north doorway and the thirteenth-century door to the south. The fourteenth-century west tower, only a little over 2 metres square internally, is in three stages with a moulded parapet and two carved gargoyles, and has a little stone octagonal spire.

Much as Norman capitals negotiate the transition from cylindrical column shaft to square abacus, the font seems to be a celebration of the transition between the square and the circle. The original moulded base is circular, as is the (restored) shaft. The inset bowl itself is a circle, but it is set in a carved square block at each corner of which a triton with two tails leans forward, clasping his tails with his hands. In the manner of the best Romanesque or Norman carving these creatures are fashioned with sufficient care to ensure their symmetry, and their subservience to the geometrical notion they serve, but characterised so that they can be understood as individual members of their curious breed. It is difficult for us to reconstruct the iconography of carvings such as these. They are at the same time deeply serious, extraordinarily inventive and often amusing. Some-times, they are apparently obscene, as in the 'sheelanagig' carving over a window of the Norman crossing tower at St Mary and St Andrew, Whittlesford, some 5 miles south of Cambridge. The medieval imagination was capable of fantastical inventions such as the 'skiapod', a creature with enormous feet which it used to shade itself from the sun.

2 The interior of the Round Church

3 The Norman font at St Peter's Church

These twin-tailed tritons, bearing their watery load, are representative of that combination of wild imagination and geometrical discipline which characterises the best of medieval art.

Notes on further reading

In this book the descriptions of architectural styles are necessarily compressed. For those seeking a more extended treatment with illustrations of important European examples, Trachtenberg and Hyman's *Architecture from Pre-History to Post-Modernism* provides a good introduction, though with an idiosyncratic treatment of post-war buildings. Of the many surveys of British architecture one of the most reliable, though now a little dated, is Kidson, Murray and Thompson, *A History of English Architecture*.

CHAPTER 3

The pattern of the colleges
(1280–1515)

UNIVERSITY AND COLLEGE

Cambridge owes its fame to its university, but the university which settled in Cambridge might well have gone elsewhere, to Stamford in Lincolnshire or Northampton, for example, both of which contained groups of scholars who had migrated from Oxford in the thirteenth century. Universities first appear in Europe during the twelfth and thirteenth centuries, independently from the medieval monasteries which were until then the only centres of learning. Though the curriculum would include grammar and rhetoric, mathematics and music, most students would concentrate on a study of theology, and as we shall see, the colleges themselves both took over monastic premises and were partly modelled on the plans of the religious houses. The University of Cambridge appears to have been founded in 1209 by scholars migrating from Oxford, which had itself received a migration of scholars from Paris in 1167. Oxford's first statutes date from 1253 and went through a number of versions until 1274 with the confirmation of the founding of Merton College. The Bishop of Ely, Hugh de Balsham, attempted to found the first college in Cambridge in 1280, by lodging students with the monks of the Hospital of St John, 'according to the rule of the scholars of Oxford called Merton', but the scholars seem to have quarrelled with their masters and in 1284 the bishop established two hostels next to the church of St Peter (now known as Little St Mary's), thus inaugurating Cambridge's first college, Peterhouse. All of the statutes and deeds of foundation, so carefully recorded in the numerous histories of the University, are retrospective – they attempt to regularise a situation which had already established itself. This is in contrast to the way in which such institutions have been founded more recently, when governments or private enterprise would conceive of a plan to answer a perceived need, and proceed to acquire land and allocate funds for capital expenditure such as building, having first calculated that income from grants or student fees will

Map 2

Ⓐ Corpus Christi College
Ⓑ Queens' College
Ⓒ Trinity College
Ⓓ Jesus College

Other buildings mentioned
① St Bene't's Church
② St Clement's Church, Bridge Street
③ St Edward's Church
④ Church of St Andrew the Less
⑤ Little St Mary's Church
⑥ St Michael's Church
⑦ Holy Trinity Church
⑧ Great St Mary's Church
⑨ Trinity Hall Library

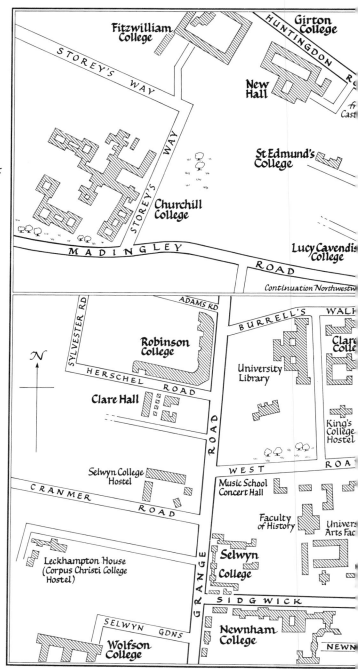

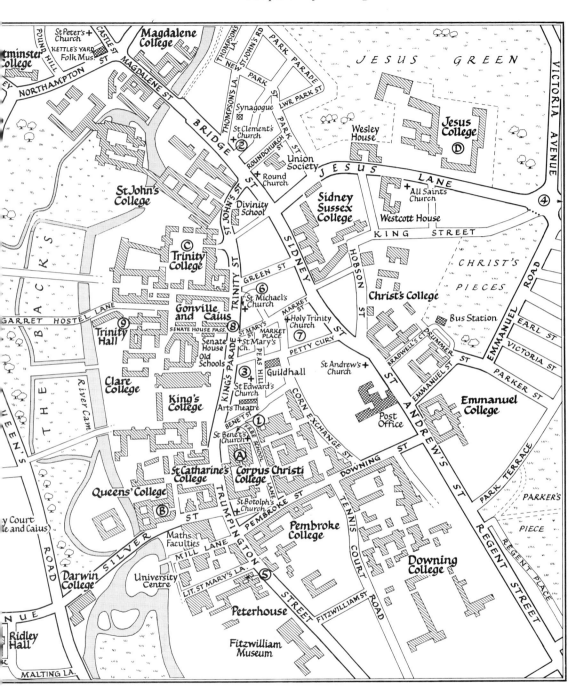

match the running costs. The haphazard organic growth in Cambridge of both University and colleges has had a profound effect upon the architecture. The University had no need for buildings because it consisted simply of the people who taught and their pupils; any reasonably large room would serve for lectures and students would live in the town in hostels and later in lodging houses. The University buildings that have appeared subsequently, mostly in the twentieth century, but beginning already with the Divinity Schools in about 1350, consist of specialised lecture theatres, offices, laboratories, and a place to conduct the ritual of the awarding of a degree. Until 1730, with the completion of Gibbs' Senate House, this had taken place in the Church of Great St Mary's. Except for the monumental University Library in west Cambridge, University buildings are still not immediately obvious.

The colleges, on the other hand, which gradually absorbed the individual hostels or lodging houses have had a more prominent physical presence. A college in Cambridge is not simply an enlarged dormitory, but an independent academic community engaged in its own research and the teaching of pupils which it has itself chosen and admitted. Colleges present their students for examination by the University (and the University will not undertake to examine anyone who is not a member of a college), and they may recommend that they attend lectures given within the University as well as teaching them within their own walls. A complex parallel academic community has emerged, where many senior members of the University are simultaneously fellows of a college (where they may conduct small group teaching or supervisions, advise students as Directors of Studies which University lectures to attend and tend to their moral welfare as Tutors) and members of a Department within a Faculty which has its own library, offices and research wing. As University lecturers they will teach and examine members of other colleges than their own. This conversion of an organic medieval system is as impossible to reduplicate in a new foundation as it has proved difficult to imitate the physical environment which has been created to serve it: a number of colleges, each with their own architectural character but participating in a similar pattern, clustered together and interspersed with University buildings, all within walking or bicycling distance of each other.

THE PATTERN OF A COLLEGE

In their monumental *Architectural History of the University of Cambridge* of 1886, Robert Willis and John Willis Clark, having outlined, at far greater length than in this volume, the foundation of the University and colleges, go on to describe each college in turn and then deal first with University buildings and finally with an analysis of the component parts of a college. They are concerned to show that the college plan does not derive directly from a monastery, and point to a striking similarity between a large country house in Derbyshire, Haddon Hall, and the plan of Queens' College (Fig. 4). It is probable that these similarities arise more because of an analogy in some aspects of the life that is contained than as direct imitation; they both have small private or shared chambers as bedrooms, for example, rather than the common dormitories of the monastery. In its enclosed defensive character the typical college also has echoes of the castle but again it is unhelpful to see the plan as deriving from this model.

The fundamental characteristic of these college buildings is that they are built around what are called quadrangles in Oxford, but invariably courts in Cambridge. The approximately rectangular court is formed by lodgings for some, but by no means all, of the scholars, both teachers and taught, a hall or dining room, a chapel (though this did not arrive immediately; Peterhouse, for instance, using the adjacent church from 1284 until 1632), a library which was often a room like any other but subsequently extended, and a Master's Lodge. The court is entered by a gate, usually with four crenellated towers, a large opening for ceremonial occasions and vehicles and a smaller one for everyday use. The space, the courtyard, is primary and the buildings are composed to form the space. Thus projections which invade the space, such as the characteristic oriel window which marks the end of the high table in the hall, are always significant, seldom merely accommodating a stair or cupboard which does not fit. As the courtyard pattern is added to, with subsequent buildings and courts, the passage between the courts assumes a special significance. In most instances it divides the hall and the kitchen, thus ensuring a cross-circulation which no functionally derived arrangement would ever have arrived at. The passage usually runs beneath a minstrels' gallery to the hall, which is open to the roof, and the timber division between the passage and the hall is known as the screens and used for college notices. The second court may be similarly enclosed, with a variety of rooms and offices, or, after the theories of Dr Caius (p. 45), three-sided. Though the courts themselves might have some planting, they are usually paved or grassed. Gardens, originally producing vegetables and fruit for the kitchens lie behind, and a Fellows' Garden is often created with an arbor or summer house, and croquet lawn. The rich architectural sequence established from street to garden, through two or more 'outdoor rooms' which become progressively more private and more rural, is capable of endless variation and rich interpretation.

GOTHIC ARCHITECTURE

This period of college building coincides with the emergence and flowering of the Gothic style of architecture. 'Gothic' was a term coined by Renaissance architects to describe anything built in the thousand-year period between the Sack of Rome by the Goths in 410 and their own rediscovery of the principles of classical architecture in the

QUEENS'
COLLEGE

SCALE OF FEET

| 10 | 0 | 10 | 20 | 30 | 40 | 50 | 60 | 70 | 80 |

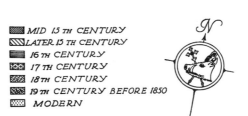

▨ MID 15 TH CENTURY
▨ LATER 15 TH CENTURY
▤ 16 TH CENTURY
▦ 17 TH CENTURY
▩ 18 TH CENTURY
▨ 19 TH CENTURY BEFORE 1850
▨ MODERN

Note:
Staircases to rooms are indicated by initial letters :- Ⓐ

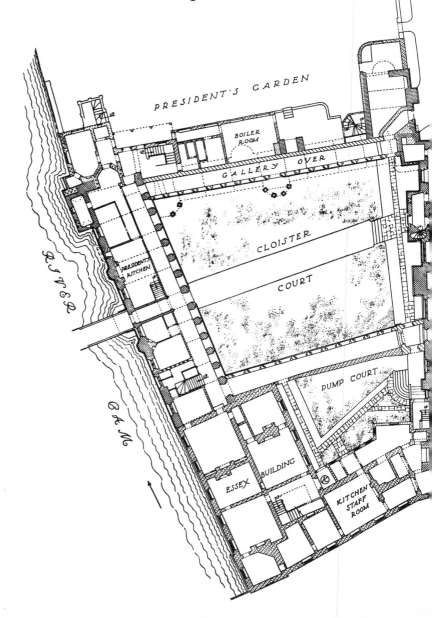

PRESIDENT'S GARDEN

BOILER ROOM

GALLERY OVER

CLOISTER

COURT

PRESIDENT'S KITCHEN

RIVER

C.K.M.

PUMP COURT

ESSEX BUILDING

Ⓡ

KITCHEN STAFF ROOM

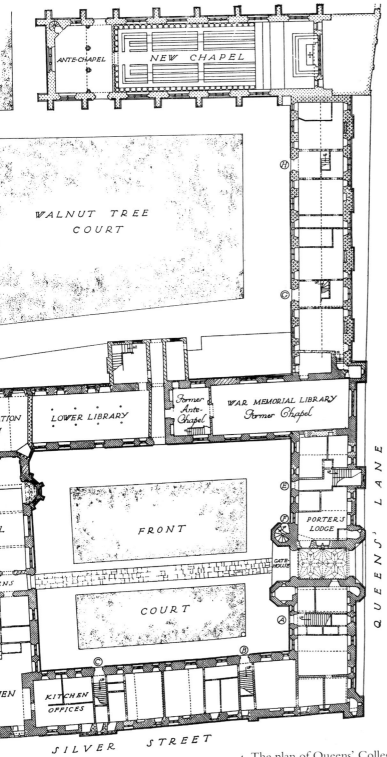

ANTE-CHAPEL

NEW CHAPEL

WALNUT TREE
COURT

Ⓗ

Ⓒ

LOWER LIBRARY

Former
Ante-
Chapel

WAR MEMORIAL LIBRARY
Former Chapel

FRONT

Ⓔ

Ⓕ

PORTER'S
LODGE

GATE-
HOUSE

COURT

Ⓐ

Ⓑ

Ⓒ

KITCHEN
OFFICES

QUEENS' LANE

SILVER STREET

4 The plan of Queens' College

early fifteenth century (described in chapter 4). It was a term of abuse, akin to the use of the word Barbarian by the Ancient Greeks to describe anyone who did not speak their own language. With few exceptions, not until the mid-eighteenth century did architects begin to look again at Gothic architecture with sympathy – at first for its exotic associations and later, in the nineteenth century, for its structural rationality and its sense of organic unity and naturalism. The emergence of the Gothic style from the Romanesque, light and skeletal rather than massive and heavy, was not merely the product of technical improvements, though without the invention of the rib vault and the flying buttress the transparency of Gothic cathedrals could not have been achieved. Nor was there just a growing aesthetic preference for dynamic linear forms. The style, as always, serves to express ideas, and Gothic architecture is pre-eminently transcendental: a Gothic cathedral is a representation of Heaven on earth and all of the technical and formal devices are means to that end.

Nineteenth-century scholars catalogued the development of English Gothic: the terminology most frequently employed is that of Thomas Rickman, whose buildings in Cambridge are discussed on p. 72. Thirteenth-century Gothic he described as 'Early English'. Windows are usually plain single-pointed arches, or lancets, and capitals have simple stylised leaves as decoration. 'Decorated' (roughly from 1290 to 1350), as its name implies, has more luxuriant foliage in its decoration; windows have organically shaped tracery and sometimes ogee heads – that is to say that the arch has a reverse curve. The Lady Chapel at Ely (about 1335–55) has 'nodding' three-dimensional ogees. Vaults become more complex, with subsidiary ribs (called 'tiercerons' and 'liernes') running between the ridges, and transverse and diagonal ribs. In France this manner is known as 'rayonnant' – like a sunburst – and there the geometry becomes freer and even more organic, culminating in 'flamboyant'. But in England, uniquely, Gothic architecture culminated in what Rickman called 'Perpendicular', a style that lasted for almost two centuries and has its final apotheosis in King's College Chapel. The complex tierceron vaults give way to the fan vault, where a dense linear pattern is spread across the whole ceiling, and window tracery becomes more rigidly divided horizontally and vertically. Almost any parish church (and those in Cambridge are no exception) will exhibit this succession of styles, though frequently the water is muddied by nineteenth-century restorers who have tried to reinstate an earlier style.

Early English examples among the town churches are the nave and aisles of St Bene't's, the nave of St Clement's, Bridge Street, and the lower part of the tower of St Edward's. But the most complete is the simple interior of St Andrew's the Less, the former chapel of the Priory at Barnwell, with its tall lancets with Purbeck marble shafts. Little St Mary's, rebuilt in the mid-fourteenth century and serving as Peterhouse's chapel until 1632, shows characteristic decorated tracery, with ogee patterns. St

24

Michael's, in Trinity Street, was used by Michaelhouse (one of the two foundations which were combined to form Trinity College) and, though plainer, is of the same period, as is the nave arcade at Holy Trinity in Market Street, but here the transepts and clerestory were added in the later fifteenth century. Great St Mary's on King's Parade is a splendid example of late Perpendicular, with delicate overall decorations between the top of the arches and the clerestory. The very shallow arches of the roof are characteristic.

CORPUS CHRISTI COLLEGE OLD COURT

Corpus Christi is unusual among Cambridge colleges in two respects. It was founded, some time between 1352 and 1355, by two town guilds, rather than by a bishop or member of the royal family or aristocracy, and it has managed in its Old Court to preserve the earliest enclosed college courtyard in the city. The Guild of Corpus Christi owned land near St Bene't's churchyard and, by a process of redevelopment and land acquisition from Gonville Hall, obtained a site between St Bene't's and St Botolph's, bounded east and west by Trumpington Street and Free School Lane. The first formal statutes were adopted in 1536; they were modelled on those of Michaelhouse of thirty years before. But the Guild of St Mary, co-founder of the college, has a history which can be traced back to 1285.

The dominant character of the college today is nineteenth-century, because in 1823–7 William Wilkins, architect of Downing College (p. 75) and the neo-Gothic screen at King's College, created his first Gothic building, confident, symmetrical and, as Pevsner says, institutional rather than collegiate. But through an arch in the northeast corner lies the Old Court, which was built between 1352 and 1378 (Fig. 5). Its appearance today is not prepossessing, and it has suffered so many alterations that little of what can be seen dates from the original construction, yet with some disentangling it can serve to illustrate the life of an undergraduate in the fourteenth century. Looking at the north range from within the court, the third archway from the left (rebuilt in 1757: the earlier four-centred arch can still be seen) was the original entrance to the college, by a passage adjacent to the churchyard of St Bene't's, where the college worshipped until about 1570. The range itself would have been simpler than it is now: there were no chimneys, and hence no heating of any kind, until the sixteenth century. The buttresses and parapets are fifteenth-century; the first-floor rooms were originally open to the roof because the second floor with its dormer windows was not installed until the sixteenth century (the present flat-headed dormers are eighteenth-century); and the openings in the fourteenth century may have been largely unglazed. The staircase partitions and of course the floors are timber-framed. All the timbers were intended to be seen but they are now hidden except in N staircase. Oliver Rackham has calculated that about 1,400 oak trees, mostly very small but totalling 100 tons of timber, were used in the construction of Old Court.

The smallest windows on the ground and first floor are original. Those on the sixth bay from the left illustrate the important pattern of single-light window adjacent to two-light window. Originally pairs of windows would light a large room from both sides of the building. This was shared by up to four students. Off this shared room would come smaller private chambers, and these are lit by the single windows. The plan for the so-called Perse and Legge building at Gonville and Caius (demolished in the nineteenth century) is a clear illustration of this pattern. On the south side of Old Court at Corpus lay the Master's Lodge, the hall, butteries and kitchen. This was the first range to be constructed and there is evidence to suggest that the hall was originally intended to be free standing. When Wilkins added New Court the old hall became the kitchens and the old kitchen and buttery was replaced by his new hall. The Perpendicular window to the old hall dates from the mid-1530s but the bay is a 1969 rebuilding of an eighteenth-century window which probably replaced a medieval half-octagon.

Passing through the archway towards Bene't Street, some of the original fourteenth-century masonry, which was rendered over on the south front in the 1920s, can be seen, most obviously in the north-east corner abutting Free School Lane. The quoins are of Barnack stone, with the main walls of thinner horizontal slabs of stone, possibly also from Barnack, near Peterborough. Joining Old Court to St Bene't's is a short range known as the Gallery, built in the Mastership of Thomas Cosyn (1487–1515). It has a single room on the ground floor and a gatehouse, inside which the remains of the springing for a quadripartite vault with moulded ribs can be detected. The surfaces of the gallery are a patchwork of brickwork and much-restored stone features, including an ogee-headed niche on the west side. The gallery appears to have been connected to the church vestry on both levels, and the upper room may have served as an oratory or small private chapel. Presumably the gateway, on to Free School Lane, also became the main entrance for the college from the early sixteenth century. Indeed, until Wilkins' nineteenth-century additions, Corpus Christi was commonly known as Bene't College.

In addition to the picture which the archaeology of the remaining buildings may help to build, the present arrangement of Corpus Christi illustrates something of the claustrophobic character of the medieval college. The generosity of the scale of Wilkins' New Court does not compensate for the loss of the Fellows' Garden, and the Master's Garden cannot be appreciated except from the splendid Master's Lodge. So the open spaces on which the rooms look are either parts of the churchyards, of St Bene't's or St Botolph's, or the enclosed courts themselves. It was this medieval sense of enclosure that Dr Caius objected to, when he came to make his New Court at Gonville and Caius (p. 45).

5 The north side of Corpus Christi College Old Court

QUEENS' COLLEGE

Queens' owes its inception to its first President, Andrew Docket, who was the Rector of St Botolph's Church and the principal of a hostel for students, St Bernard's. In 1446 he obtained a Royal Charter to incorporate his hostel into a college. On 15 April 1448 Queen Margaret of Anjou, Henry VI's wife, issued a charter founding 'The Queen's College of St Margaret and St Bernard' and the building of Front Court began immediately. Queen Elizabeth, the wife of Henry VI's rival, Edward IV, became the college's patroness, at the request of Docket, and the patronage of successive Queens of England is celebrated in the spelling Queens' rather than Queen's.

In contrast to Corpus Christi, the design of Queens', and in particular Front Court, is sophisticated and self-conscious. The architect was almost certainly Reginald Ely, a friend and parishioner of the first President, and we also know the name of the carpenter for the woodwork, Thomas Sturgeon from Elsenham in Essex. The plan, reproduced on pp. 22–3, indicates the characteristic collegiate arrangement, already briefly described. The gatehouse, which was constructed first with the east range, has octagonal turrets on each corner, one of which contains a spiral stair, on the pattern of the Edward II tower at Trinity of 1430. This motif, with its embattled parapets, is derived from the medieval castle, but had already been adopted in large houses for display rather than defence, and was to find its grandest expression in the gates to the Royal Palace at Hampton Court. The Porter's Lodge controls the entrance, and above it sits the muniment room, or treasury, containing the college's most precious possessions. It has a quadripartite vault, and the gateway itself has an original two-bay ribbed stone vault with liernes and carved bosses depicting, appropriately, St Margaret and St Bernard at the principal intersections. As in cathedrals, stone vaulting not only celebrates the importance of the space, in this case the threshold to the college, but also acts as fire protection to the fabric. Either side of the gate, the east range exhibits an alternation of two-light and single-light windows reflecting the original room layout described in relation to Corpus Christi Old Court. Much has been restored, and even re-restored. The eaves, for instance, reproduce the way that Loggan, in the seventeenth century, recorded the college, but in the eighteenth and early nineteenth centuries a battlemented parapet had been installed. The hall opposite was constructed as soon as the east and south ranges had been completed (a contract for the woodwork is dated March 1449). The oriel window (with its own lierne-vault inside) marks the division between the high-table dais and the rest of the room, which is centred on a large fireplace. Behind the 1732 pedimented panelling at the north end lies the Fellows' combination room and a connection to the President's Lodge in the next court, while to the south, separated by the screens passage, is the kitchen. This pattern echoes that of innumerable medieval manor houses, where the hall represents the principal gathering space for the whole household, with the master of the house and his entourage (in this case President and Fellows) approaching from one side, and the rest of the inhabitants (here, undergraduates) from the other. The element of theatricality involved in the ritual of dining is recalled as much by the decorated panelling and stage-like dais as it is in the Latin grace at the start of a meal, after the entry of the gowned members of the high table. Bodley (an important nineteenth-century architect whose work is discussed in chapter 6) restored the hall in 1858–62, and redecorated it with William Morris' firm in 1875.

On the north side of Front Court lay the library and chapel; in 1858–61 Bodley refitted the chapel, removing a plaster ceiling installed in the eighteenth century, and replacing it with a copy of what was originally there. In 1890 he was employed to build a new chapel, and in the twentieth century the old chapel has been subdivided and fitted out as a library. The large painted sundial with the signs of the zodiac is mid-seventeenth-century in origin. The old library is on the first floor of the west part of the north range, and retains its original moulded ceiling, beams and broad oak planks on the floor. It has five projecting bookcases, originally from the sixteenth century but heightened in the eighteenth century, and represents in miniature a typical college library. (Of the many on this pattern in Cambridge, the library at Trinity Hall is the least altered.) Bookcases lie at right angles to the windows and create bays for study, leaving a passage down the centre of the room. This clear arrangement allows a measure of privacy to each well-lit bay and good side-lighting on to the book spines. The rhythm of the furnishings (bookcases and tables) is in step with the structure (window openings and exposed beams). It is an arrangement with monastic precedent, and many subsequent modifications: from Wren's Trinity Library with its U-shaped bays (p. 60) to Cockerell's monumental Old University Library (p. 78). In very large collections such as Scott's 1922 University Library (p. 95), catalogue areas, bookstacks and study spaces cannot have such a privileged close co-existence, but it is interesting to see in some late twentieth-century college libraries, such as that at Jesus College by Evans and Shalev, the same pattern re-appearing.

West of Front Court, and connected by the screens passage, lies Queens' Cloister Court; it was begun even before the completion of Front Court, so that unlike many other colleges where the second court is an accretion, Queens' was always conceived of as a two-court arrangement. But the irregular shape and more varied appearance indicate a more complex history. The western range was built first, much on the pattern of Front Court, and was joined with cloisters to the other buildings at the very end of the fifteenth century. William of Wykeham had introduced cloisters at New College, Oxford, a hundred years before and in that city there are grand cloistered quadrangles also at Magdalen and Christ Church but in Cambridge, apart from this court at Queens', there are only eighteenth- or nineteenth-century arcades. The picturesque timber-framed long gallery over the north cloister was not built until the late sixteenth century though there may have been an earlier superstructure. The brackets holding the timber upper floors are placed with complete disregard to the rhythm of the brick arches below. The closely spaced timbers were exposed originally, then rendered over, and only re-emerged in a repair of 1911. The spiral staircase on the north-east is Elizabethan while the gallery itself is entirely panelled with later sixteenth- or early seventeenth-century oak. Heraldic glass in the south-facing bay window is partly sixteenth-century and partly nineteenth. Elizabethan houses often had long galleries, rooms for exercise in inclement weather and the display of portraits. Here the gallery connects the President's lodging with the dais end of the college's hall and so it is in a sense an enlarged corridor. But until the nineteenth century internal spaces for 'circulation' as a separate activity did not exist: one went from room to room. The passage-like gallery, with its splendid central fireplace, is equally suitable for relatively intimate gatherings in the centre of the space as for a larger standing congregation of people preparatory to a dinner.

James Essex's mid-eighteenth-century building at the south-west corner of Cloister Court, twice as deep as any of the other buildings, replaced a 1564 clunch and stone building. The 'mathematical' timber bridge over the Cam, despite many misleading myths, was built in 1904 and is a copy of the bridge that was constructed in 1749–50 by James Essex to the design of W. Etheridge.

Queens' expanded north-west in the nineteenth century and over the Cam in the twentieth, building over large parts of its gardens with new accommodation, sports facilities and a dining hall. Because the centre of gravity of the college has shifted, the two old courts, well preserved as they are, have something of a museum quality.

TRINITY COLLEGE

On 7 July 1317, Edward II issued a writ directing the Sheriff of Cambridgeshire to provide a hostel for up to thirteen children from the Royal Household. Eleven of them arrived two days later and by 1319 the number of scholars housed had risen to thirty-two. Edward III regularised the hostel with a proper endowment and in 1337 it was named King's Hall. It was at that time the largest college in Cambridge and was sited on what is now Trinity Street. Statutes survive from 1380 and show that scholars had to be at least 14 years old with sufficient Latin to study logic or other subjects prescribed by the Warden. Only Latin or French could be spoken at mealtimes; until 1485 the scholars worshipped in the Church of All Saints (destroyed in the nineteenth century and replaced by Bodley's church in Jesus Lane, p. 82). In 1546 King's Hall, at the insistence of Henry VIII, surrendered its statutes to become Trinity College. Trinity also swallowed up Physwick Hostel and Michaelhouse, a smaller but well-endowed foundation of 1324 of Harvey de Stanton, situated a little to the south-west. The new college used the relatively recently constructed chapel of King's Hall and the dining hall of Michaelhouse, and the Warden of King's Hall became the first Master of Trinity. New rooms, a library and the chapel were erected between 1555 and 1567 but we owe the present pattern of Trinity College to the vision and energy of Thomas Nevile who was Master between 1593 and 1615. During an eight-year building campaign at the end of the sixteenth century he re-fashioned the jumble of previous courts to create the large, irregular but serene space of Trinity Great Court (Fig. 6). This involved demolition of recent as well as older buildings, and moving wholesale King Edward's Tower, originally part of Michaelhouse, back to line with the chapel. This, Queen Mary I's only major building project, is in a plain late Perpendicular style with a very shallow pitch to its internal ceiling. The screens and stalls are later.

It is extraordinary to realise that this chapel was built at about the time of Michelangelo's death: stylistically at the transition between Mannerism and Baroque (see chapter 4). But a building's architectural quality has little to do with whether it

6 Trinity Great Court: hall, fountain and chapel

reflects continental fashions, and the same could be said for urbanism, because it is the creation of Great Court that is Nevile's great achievement – one of the memorable urban spaces in Europe. As at Piazza San Marco in Venice, or the Campo in Siena, the individual buildings that surround the space are of different ages and unequal quality. Nevile made his own gate, on the east side towards Trinity Street. It is on the same pattern as the rebuilt King Edward's Tower, which when originally constructed was the first gatehouse in Cambridge and set the pattern for the subsequent gates. Nevile's Great Gate is larger and broader, of brick with stone quoins and castellations. It has a single arch to the court, but two separate openings to the east, rather than a door within a door which is more normal in Cambridge. The large doorway is opened on ceremonial occasions, such as the arrival of a new Master, who has to knock on the gate and be admitted by the Fellows, or visits by Royalty. Prince Charles was entertained by Thomas Nevile in 1613, and in 1615 James I made two visits. The façade is embellished by crude statuary. Through the gateway, one steps down into the court, rather like entering a great room. The principal way out, via the screens, lies diagonally across the grassed irregular square, but the view of this is blocked by the three-storey fountain. Most of the courtyard is made up of three-storey ranges of rooms on the familiar staircase arrangement, some rendered, some stone faced. On the north side the three floors rise straight to a battlemented parapet (this used to be the library) but on the south and east the second floor has dormer windows set behind a parapet, giving a surprisingly domestic two-storey scale to the long ranges. The Master's Lodge, opposite, is similar, but with a prominent bay and gable added by Salvin in the nineteenth century. The chapel, on the north side, and the hall with its great oriel and enormously enlarged scale, are obvious; the latter is the largest in Cambridge and was based on Middle Temple Hall in London, of thirty years earlier, with a hammer-beam roof, oriel windows facing both east and west, and a splendid lantern.

The south side of Great Court (the first stage of Nevile's building works) has its own gateway, Queen's Gate, and, on the façade facing Trinity Lane, a remarkable enfilade of chimneys, most effective when seen obliquely from Trinity Street and much admired by the Finnish architect Alvar Aalto when he visited Cambridge in the 1950s. To the south, the combination room was altered and re-faced by James Essex in 1774 in a plain Georgian style. Semicircular steps lead down from the screens and through into the second court, named after Thomas Nevile, at the far side of which stands the library by Christopher Wren (described on pp. 60–2).

The large irregular shape of Great Court and the heterogeneous collection of buildings possess an unforgettable dignity, which has provoked a number of rituals that seem to celebrate its character. The 'Great Court run' involves a race around the perimeter of the court, while the clock (which was accurately described by Wordsworth, an undergraduate of neighbouring St John's, as 'loquacious') strikes twelve, which it does first in a low register and then again on a higher note. The semicircular steps up to the hall are also the site of energetic attempts to leap up the full flight. But perhaps the elaborate fountain (1601–15 but rebuilt in 1715) is the key to the special character of the court: its original function, of bringing water to the ranges of rooms which had none until the nineteenth century, is long superseded, but the continuous background trickle of water in the centre of this huge court effectively suppresses the noise of anything but immediate conversation. So it not only acts visually, as an effective sculptural centrepiece to the space of the court, but audibly inhabits it. In a narrow sense, this structure is now functionally useless, yet Trinity Great Court can hardly be imagined without it. Function must always have a wider definition than mere utility but, as Alberti, the great Renaissance architect, pointed out, architecture is 'born of necessity, nourished by convenience, dignified by use; and only in the end is pleasure provided for'.

JESUS COLLEGE

Though, as we have seen, Jesus is far from the oldest college, it has some claims to be in another sense the most 'ancient' of the colleges – the age of its origin being greater than that of the University itself. Its un-collegiate, monastic plan is explained by the fact that it was founded, as was mentioned (p. 10), in the twelfth century as a convent. A charter of 1133 from Nigellus, the second Bishop of Ely, refers to 'the nuns of the little cell lately instituted without the town of Cantebruge'. Some of Jesus College's properties in outlying villages were bequeathed at that time, more than 850 years ago. The name of the college, properly 'The College of the Blessed Mary the Virgin, St John the Evangelist, and the glorious Virgin St Radegund' indicates its origin: the convent church which was constructed between 1159 and 1161 on land given to the nuns by King Malcolm IV of Scotland, the Earl of Huntingdon, was dedicated to St Mary; there was a chapel to St Radegund, who had founded the Abbey of the Holy Cross at Poitiers which Malcolm had visited in 1159. In 1250 what is now partly occupied as the college Chapel was the largest church in Cambridge, at about 58 metres in length, but in 1277 the bell-tower fell and there were disastrous fires in 1313 and 1376.

On 12 June 1496 the Bishop of Ely, John Alcock, under licence from Henry VII, dissolved the convent, which by then consisted of two nuns only, one of whom was described as 'infamis', or of ill reputation. The prioress' house became the Master's Lodge; her apartment is now called the Prioress' Room. The Norman convent church became, in part, the chapel. A fragment of the cloister at the entrance to what was the chapter house is still visible (Fig. 7). Its level is lower than Essex's eighteenth-century brick cloister and is lowered further by steps which would have increased the relative height of the chapter house, beneath the uniform floor of the nuns' dormitory above. Alcock was Controller of the Royal Works and Buildings under Henry VII and built at Ely and Great St Mary's in Cambridge. The architectural scheme for the adaptation of the nunnery buildings appears to be his even though he died only four years later in 1500. Part of the nave of the church he converted for rooms, and he further reduced the building by pulling down chapels on the north and south sides of the choir and giving its northern aisles to the cloister: the original columns can be seen embedded in the wall. At the same time he re-roofed the church at a lower pitch and inserted large windows in the Perpendicular style. He also re-roofed the hall in Spanish chestnut and faced up the clunch (or chalky stone) walls of the rest of the nunnery with brick. Finally, by re-dedicating the church in the name of Jesus he gave the college its name.

Fragments of Bishop Alcock's furnishings remain in the chapel, notably in the bench end south of the chancel screen door. Alcock is shown kneeling. A cockerel on a globe stands next to him, is seen again in the crook of his staff and surmounts the canopy above him. This is Alcock's 'rebus' – a simple pun on the two syllables of his name, the globe standing for 'all'. Alcock's rebus is to be found throughout the college and Jesus, which still supports a 'roosters' club, has an enviable collection of silver and bronze cockerels including an eighteenth-century one from Benin, donated in 1897.

But much of what one now sees in the chapel is the result of nineteenth-century restorations beginning in 1844 when eighteenth-century accretions were removed along with Alcock's low-pitched roof, which Pugin (see p. 73) replaced with a high-pitched one in thirteenth-century style. He also removed the Perpendicular east window and replaced it with three tall lancets; there was some archaeological evidence that he was thereby restoring the original pattern. Further repairs were carried out by Bodley in 1864–7. He was working on All Saints', over the road (see p. 82). The stained glass and painted ceiling, by Burne-Jones and William Morris respectively, date from a further restoration beginning in 1873.

The chapel and its immediate surroundings therefore make an excellent place to indulge in architectural detective-work. The earliest parts are Norman; there are fragments of authentic Early English, Decorated and Perpendicular; Essex's eighteenth-century cloisters remain but inevitably there is much nineteenth-century work. This, however, is of a very high order and does succeed in retaining and enhancing the character of this remarkable building.

In the hall, the former first-floor refectory of the nunnery, Alcock's chestnut roof can be seen, and a beautiful north-facing oriel window, both of which were repaired by Waterhouse in 1868. The pattern of the tracery is carried over on to the stone walls at either side of the projection and up into the arch. More elaborate tracery occurs over the oriel itself. Bishop Alcock's library, now the college Old Library, retains its original ceiling and arrangement as at Queens' or Trinity Hall. The bookcases, however, are seventeenth-century. Bishop Alcock's ubiquitous rebus can be seen in the stained glass.

In contrast to Queens', Jesus like many of the other colleges has little of the museum about it, but this has other consequences. The difficulty of installing modern catering equipment and servicing what was formerly the kitchen of a convent 'without the town' is only one example of the sacrifice of convenience that must be accepted if historic fabric is to be maintained in daily use: food deliveries are made by hand-pulled trolley across several hundred metres of paving and cobbles from the nearest place accessible by road.

Notes on further reading

For a general account of English Gothic, and indeed Norman, see Alec Clifton-Taylor's *The Cathedrals of England*.

Most of the colleges have their own histories, in addition to the general books noted at the end of chapter 1. The Cambridgeshire Collection at the Central Library in Cambridge has a

7 Jesus College: Early English arches at the entrance to the chapter house of the former convent of St Radegund

comprehensive collection of books and articles. For Queens' see J. Twigg (1987), for Corpus Patrick Bury (1949 and 1952), and for Trinity G.M Trevelyan (1943 and 1983) and R. Robson (1967). There is a history of Jesus College by Arthur Gray and Frederick Brittain, and of the chapel, written in 1914, by Iris and Gerda Morgan. Oliver Rackham's calculations of timbers used in the construction of Old Court, together with a convincing interpretation of its construction, are in the Letters of the Corpus Association, nos. 66 and 67.

For the story of the assembly of the land to build Peterhouse, see the article by Hall and Lovatt in the *Proceedings of the Cambridge Antiquarian Society*, 78 (1989), which points out that the conventional collegiate arrangement did not arrive until the middle of the fourteenth century; Peterhouse's unusual arrangement, with the hall and screens not opposite the main entrance, is accounted for by the pattern of land acquisition.

CHAPTER 4

The English Renaissance in Cambridge (1515–1663)

THE CLASSICAL LANGUAGE

The four examples studied in this chapter represent the absorption in England of the Renaissance style of architecture which had originated in Italy. In order to understand the motifs and elements of the architecture it is necessary briefly to explain the nature of classical architecture. We can identify a classical building (as opposed to a Gothic building) most easily by recognising these motifs, in particular the 'five orders' described below, but classical architecture does not consist only in its decorative elements, or rather its elements are more than decorative. As the word 'orders' suggests it also constitutes a formal system for arranging the disposition of the parts of the building on plan, section and elevation. The orders themselves derive from Greek and Roman building practice and were described in the only treatise to survive from antiquity, *De Architectura* by Marcus Pollio Vitruvius (active 46–30 BC in Rome). Vitruvius' book was not printed until 1486 but was known in manuscript by Alberti, the most important early Renaissance architect and theoretician whose own *De re Aedificatoria* (completed in manuscript in 1452 and first printed 1485) is closely modelled on it. The concept of a formal ordering system also derives from Greece and Rome, from Aristotle's *The Art of Rhetoric* and *Poetics* where the techniques and rules of composition are described as devices to affect the understanding and emotions of the recipients of a given art form, principles that were reiterated in the work of later Roman writers, such as Cicero. The rediscovery by Alberti and others in Florence in the mid-fifteenth century of these classical principles was, of course, only a part of the immense cultural upheaval of the Renaissance. In architecture the compositional rules may be summarised as the regular disposition of parts (usually as an orthogonal grid system); a tripartite division of each element (at its most basic, a beginning, middle and end, usually with the stress on the middle section); and a placing of the elements in a coherent (usually symmetrical)

37

Map 3

Ⓐ King's College Chapel screen
Ⓑ Gonville and Caius College
   Gate of Honour
Ⓒ Christ's College Fellows' Building
Ⓓ Clare College

Other buildings mentioned
① Peterhouse chapel
② Magdalene College Pepys Library
③ Trinity College, hall and fountain
④ St John's College, 1792 bridge

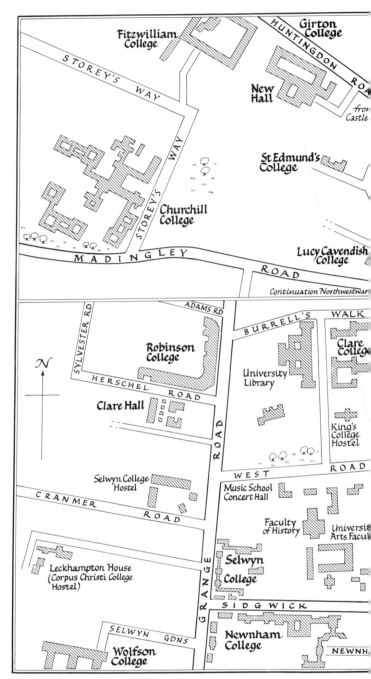

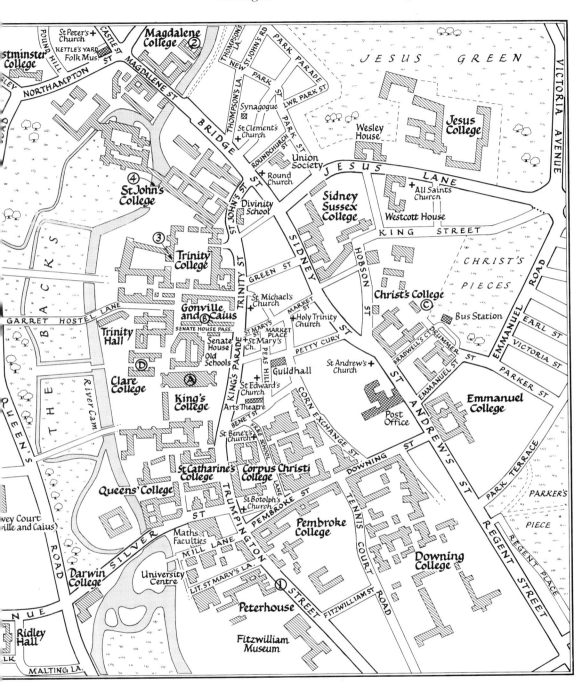

relation to one another. The most important of the elements were the orders and it is the choice of order and the way it is disposed which governs the composition and character of a classical building.

Figure 8 illustrates the five orders in a woodcut from the First Book of *L'Architettura* by Sebastiano Serlio, a painter and architect born in Bologna in 1475, three years after Alberti's death. Serlio's books were immensely influential throughout Europe and his codification of the orders became the model for many other textbooks. From left to right, he shows Tuscan, Doric, Ionic, Corinthian and Composite. The three central orders are Greek derived; Tuscan and Composite are Roman inventions. The orders have widely varying proportions, from the sturdy Tuscan and Doric to the more slender Ionic and graceful, richly decorated Corinthian and Composite. Their proportions (the rules for which were minutely prescribed in successive handbooks) imply not only character (sturdy/graceful) but also anthropomorphism such that the Ionic order can be replaced in a Greek temple by the statue of a young girl (Caryatid) and the Doric by a statue of a giant (Atlantid). The orders appear as free-standing columns in Serlio's illustration but they may also be attached to (or 'engaged with') the wall or even flattened against it, as pilasters. One way in which classical buildings can be read is therefore as a formal system of geometric and proportional refinement; another, perhaps subliminally, is by a process of empathy whereby we substitute ourselves, as it were, for the column which is carrying the load of the beam above, or framing a significant doorway. Each column exhibits in itself a classical tripartite subdivision (base, shaft and capital) and the beam or entablature which they carry is again divided into three (architrave, frieze and cornice) each element of which, in turn, has a further triple subdivision. The vertical incisions in the frieze of the Doric order (triglyphs) were claimed by Vitruvius to be representations in stone of the ends of the timber beams which formed the first Greek temples. The characteristic scrolls of the Ionic capital are supposed to derive from rams' horns and the foliage in the capital of the Corinthian order is formed of acanthus leaves. There are therefore natural (animal and vegetable) analogies embedded in the orders, and these associations too can be used in the composition of classical buildings.

Art historians have identified a number of phases of Italian Renaissance classicism, in architecture as well as painting. The 'High Renaissance', the period when the classical language is used in its purest and most developed form, occurs in Rome between about 1500 and 1520. There is a careful balance between the composition of masses and the application of decoration. 'Mannerism' in the sixteenth century describes the 'maniera' or style of architects trained in the classical language who apply its vocabulary in an

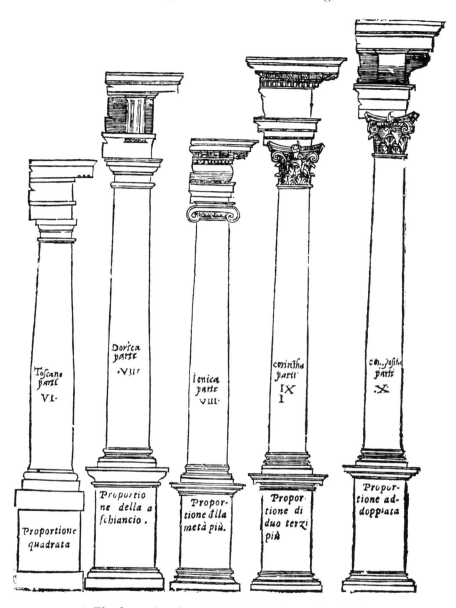

8 The five orders, from Serlio's *L'Architettura*, First Book

apparently arbitrary or illogical way. An expectation of a particular composition is established, only to be contradicted. This has been seen both as a reaction to a society and culture where authentic architectural forms can no longer be limited to those which favour poise and harmony, and as the over-sophisticated use of the language as a kind of joke which educated patrons might be expected to enjoy. With the Counter-Reformation, in the late sixteenth and early seventeenth centuries, architecture serves a new end in expressing the power of the Catholic Church and the authority of individual patrons, and in the Baroque style the classical Renaissance coherence and the grammatical freedom gained in Mannerism are welded together by an iconographic programme into works of powerful theatrical effect. As usual, these distinctions are only helpful in so far as they assist us in appreciating better the work of individual architects such as Michelangelo or Palladio whose buildings defy such categorisation.

CLASSICAL ARCHITECTURE COMES TO CAMBRIDGE

Inigo Jones (1573–1652) is the British architect credited with bringing a fully developed Italianate classical style to England. Though he designed the Prince's Lodging (now destroyed) at Newmarket he built nothing in Cambridge. But we do have the central portion of a choir screen he made for Winchester Cathedral. It is on the upper floor of T. G. Jackson's archaeology museum in Downing Street (p. 92). Whereas his predecessors and his contemporaries in England mostly absorbed the motifs, usually from pattern-books, as a decorative overlay to a building which was substantially medieval in pattern, Jones understood classicism in all its complexity and subtlety.

The brief description of orthodox classicism above serves its first purpose in pointing out how unclassical many of the manifestations of classicism in Cambridge are. A visit to the chapel at Peterhouse would illustrate the point. The galleries either side of the chapel, seen from the west, are supported on round arches with an engaged Tuscan Doric order, but the proportions of base to column are quite bizarre if they are compared to Serlio's prescription (Fig. 8). Although the cloisters were entirely rebuilt in 1709, we know from Loggan's print that similar columns had originally framed Perpendicular, pointed arches like those across the front of the chapel, when they had been erected between 1635 and 1644. In chapter 5 we shall compare this building with the first of Christopher Wren's three buildings in Cambridge, the chapel for Pembroke College, just across Trumpington Street.

The Pepys Library at Magdalene College is another building of the period worth studying. It is U-shaped, with its open court facing north-east towards the Fellows' Garden, but it presents itself to Magdalene's second court as if it were an H, because the roofs have been returned at either end to form two gables which flank an open ground-floor arcade. They are just 300 mm in front of the wall-plane of the rest of the building.

KING'S COLLEGE CHAPEL — THE CHANCEL STALLS AND SCREEN

The chapel at King's (1446–1515) is probably the pre-eminent architectural masterpiece in the city, and certainly the most visited. Whole books have been devoted to the building and its magnificent stained glass. This description concentrates on a massive piece of furniture within the chapel, the chancel stalls and screen which were erected fifteen to twenty years after the chapel itself was complete (Fig. 9). Where the style of the chapel is one of the finest examples of Perpendicular, the final and most characteristically English flowering of the Gothic manner, the woodwork is purely Renaissance. The extraordinary contrast that this creates was somewhat diluted by the insertion of Rubens' *Adoration of the Magi*, a seventeenth-century Baroque masterpiece, in the 1960s, but there is still a vivid conjunction between the two. It is immediately apparent that although proportionally the stalls, and especially the screen, are convincingly correct, every part of the woodwork has been decorated and worked over. The ornamentation includes heads in the roundels above the arches in the screen, cherubs, animals and birds and stylised plant forms all woven within the panels of the pilasters, friezes and covings of the woodwork. Some of the elements are later, such as the canopies over the stalls and the north door which carries a date of 1636, but the style is remarkably consistent. The elaborate coats of arms on the backs of the side stalls and St George and the Dragon with figures above and below are especially rich. Scholars have argued over who executed this carving. Since the style is so advanced and the ornamentation relates to contemporary examples in Holland and France but is unparalleled in England, it has been supposed that the artists were foreign.

The classical style was disseminated through Europe by the patronage of monarchs, notably François I at Fontainebleau (1528). The generation of architects who came to France, Spain and the Netherlands were pupils of the great High Renaissance architects and the style they employed was, by Italian standards, impure. Whereas many of the early Renaissance houses in England, such as Burghley House for Lord Cecil, near Stamford, and as we shall see several important buildings in Cambridge also, are 'Mannerist' before they are 'classical', it is remarkable that this screen, despite its elaborate ornamentation, retains to our eyes a classic sense of order. The repetitive round arches, the subdivisions of base, shaft and entablature, and the careful hierarchy of the composition ensure that the effect which could so easily become overwhelming and chaotic is nevertheless rich and sober, exuberant yet dignified. Many of the college chapels have later eighteenth-century screens and woodwork where the carving is much less ornate, and dignity is achieved by restraint, an easier path to pursue than the balancing act achieved at King's. In its own manner it attains an authority to match that of the late Gothic masterpiece within which it is situated. To emphasise this it is only necessary to compare other large-scale carving work in Cambridge. One example is the

9 The stalls and chancel screen in King's College Chapel

oak screen in the hall at Trinity College. This was erected at the beginning of the seventeenth century, and, appropriately for a dining hall rather than a chapel, the flamboyance of the decoration pervades the whole form of the screen. Columns are entwined with foliage and the pilasters are wider at the top than the bottom. Strapwork imitation of leather decoration can also be seen on the wonderful fountains in the centre of Great Court, Trinity College, and at the start of Hobson's Conduit on Trumpington Street.

GONVILLE AND CAIUS COLLEGE GATE OF HONOUR

The Gate of Honour at Caius is not only a delightful building in itself but together with its companions, the gates of Humility and Virtue, represents as clearly as any other example in Cambridge the way that an iconographic programme can order the physical fabric of the architecture to structure and give meaning to the activities of those who use the buildings, both day-to-day and on special occasions (Fig. 10).

Dr Caius was elected Master of his old college Gonville Hall in 1559 after he had re-founded it with a considerable donation two years earlier. Gonville Hall had originally only a single court, entered off Trinity Lane to its north, and the new Master created Caius Court on garden land to the south. Later, buildings were added, up to Trinity Street on the east side. These were replaced by Waterhouse to form the present Tree Court in 1870 (see p. 81). Caius, who latinised his name from 'Keys' which remains its correct pronunciation, was familiar with French and Italian classical architecture, because he had studied medicine at Padua and had visited Rome, Florence and Bologna on his way back to England. As President of the College of Physicians and physician to both Edward VI and Queen Mary, he was also concerned above all for the health of his students and fellows. His new court was therefore U-shaped, open towards the south to let in sunlight and air ('lest the air, from being confined within a narrow space, should become foul', as he writes) with only the wall and the Gate of Honour dividing the college from the former School Street, now Senate House Passage. This gate is the final and most elaborate of the three which Caius erected as part of his building campaign. The first, towards Trinity Street, now stands in the Master's Garden, and is the Gate of Humility. Waterhouse's rebuilding in the nineteenth century retained the inscription 'Humilitatis' over his east gateway, so that the iconographic programme is maintained. For this is the gate through which the aspiring student would first be expected to come. Between Tree Court and Caius Court is the Gate of Virtue: through this the students would pass daily, and gain thereby in both virtue and wisdom, since the western face has the inscription 'Io Caius Posuit Sapientiae 1567'. The Gate of Honour marks the point of exit from the college to the world outside and in particular to the schools where the student would sit his

10 Gonville and Caius College Gate of Honour with the Old University Library beyond

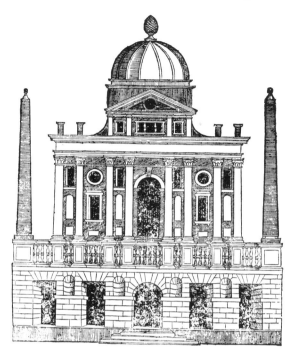

11 Two plates from Serlio's *L'Architettura*, Fourth Book

University examinations. Thus it celebrates the most significant rite of passage through the institution. At one level the gates are strictly functional, and Dr Caius' instructions (in College Statutes 29 and 52) are quite specific as to the hours in which they should be opened and closed for the convenience and safety of his students, 'lest persons . . . purloin articles of property that have been left lying about: and turn a private path into a public thoroughfare by the prescription of long use'. At another level, however, the gate in the wall which can be closed and opened with specific ceremony offers the opportunity for ritual of a moving kind. To this day, after the funeral of a Fellow of the college, the service taking place in the chapel on the north side of Caius Court, the door (unexpectedly locked in daytime) is opened to allow the coffin to be borne through the Gate of Honour to a waiting hearse, equally surprisingly occupying the passage which is normally reserved for cyclists and pedestrians.

The detailed architecture of the gate is most extraordinary in its scale. It is a diminutive structure, with an intricacy of ornament more often found in furniture. Its elevations are quite closely modelled on two examples in Book IV of Sebastiano Serlio's *L'Architettura,* which appeared in six parts between 1537 and 1551 (Fig. 11). Book IV is in many respects the most important part, because it deals with the orders and 'by them the whole Art [of architecture] is learned', as Serlio noted in the preface. The particular plates on which the design is modelled (51, which has the curved side pieces that Alberti and other Italian architects had used on the façades of their churches and 55 which sports four obelisks) are in the eighth chapter, dealing with the Corinthian order. It is because Dr Caius has chosen, as an enrichment to his Gate of Honour, examples of whole temple or church fronts rather than of gateways in the Corinthian manner, of which there are a number illustrated, that the scale is so distorted. The complete iconography would take many chapters to unravel, but it is worth mentioning one other fact. According to the College Annals and recorded in Loggan's print of about 1688, Caius Court had a column in its centre erected by Theodore Haveus of Cleves which acted as a huge gnomon and contained no fewer than sixty sundials. Willis and Clark surmise that the form of the main dial was a hexecontahedron. This little south-facing courtyard was not only conceived of as healthy and secure, but suffused with symbolism that encompassed geometry and the elements as well as the passage of the students from first induction to graduation.

CHRIST'S COLLEGE FELLOWS' BUILDING

The First Court of Christ's is based on the former 'Grammar College of God's House' and, though much altered in the eighteenth and nineteenth centuries, retains its sixteenth-century form and atmosphere. Behind lies the Fellows' Building – a bold free-standing structure in its own garden (Fig. 12). We read it as an object in space,

12 Christ's College Fellows' Building

rather than as part of a wall defining an enclosed space, and this interpretation is underlined by the emphatic corners with their giant Ionic pilasters. Its overall form would have seemed, in the mid-seventeenth century, as 'modern' as its decoration. The motifs on the façade are those that can also be found in Elizabethan houses by Robert Smythson (such as Wollaton Hall and Longleat): cross-shaped stone mullions, triangular and curved pediments, a balustrade rather than a gutter at the eaves, as well as the use of the orders. The anonymous designer (certainly not Inigo Jones and probably not Thomas Grumbold, whose work at Clare College has some similarities with this building) must have been familiar with the pattern-books of Serlio (see above for the way in which Caius College Gate of Honour refers to the plates in Serlio's 1537 Fourth Book), but the building is at the same time unmistakably English in its character of robustness, playfulness and naïveté. There is no classical precedent for the little semicircular hiccups between the open balustrades in front of the dormer windows. The use of the giant order carrying through several storeys is usually described as an invention of Michelangelo (though examples appear almost simultaneously in England at Kirby Hall in Northamptonshire), while the alternation of triangular and curved pediments, also used by Michelangelo, Sangallo and others, is taken to extreme lengths: it creates a bouncy rhythm to the eleven dormer windows across the length of the façade and avoids vertical repetition over each of the entrances (round – pointed – round on the ground floor; pointed – round – pointed on the first floor). There are the same subtle manipulations of the wall-plane that we have noticed in the Pepys Building at Magdalene, here involving the very shallow projections of the entrance bays. The classical motifs are used not as a proportional ordering device but (most obviously at the corner Ionic pilasters) as emblems of modernity. It is therefore quite possible for the designer to widen the central entrance and give it a four-centred (almost Perpendicular) arch under the pointed pediment which only manages to fit beneath the window cill above because that window, uniquely on the first floor, has four panes over four panes rather than four over six. As we shall see (p. 55) at Emmanuel College Wren solved a similar problem with similar means, but in his case the more 'correct' classical language employed creates a more obvious discord. The proportions of bases to column shafts at the door surrounds are not as extremely unclassical as at Peterhouse chapel (p. 42) but they would still be regarded as amateur by a French or Italian visitor. Around the ground-floor windows are rustications – blocks of stone invade the more delicate window architraves forming what was, in the eighteenth century, to be known as a Gibbs surround after James Gibbs (see p. 65). The keystones and the blocks either side, at the head of each window, are flush with the stone string course, and run into it at first-floor level, almost as if they were hung from it, and this has the effect of binding together the whole ground floor and establishing a base for the first-floor 'piano nobile'. Since the string course projects by the same amount as the base, it is almost possible to read the wall-plane on the ground floor as having been cut out of a greater thickness of stone.

While the style could be called 'Mannerist', as defined in the brief description of classical architecture earlier in this chapter (p. 40), its effect is not of a knowing and self-conscious game, nor is it merely clumsy and provincial. As so often in the best of English architecture, we are in the presence of a designer who is struggling to create a noble and dignified building and drawing upon a variety of motifs towards that end. Unconstrained by rules, the invention is nevertheless subtle.

It is interesting to see how a subsequent generation has interpreted this building. For the eighteenth-century classical architect it would seem ignorant, but by the late nineteenth century buildings such as these were admired precisely for their robust Englishness. W. R. Lethaby (the founder of the Central School of Art and Design) wrote appreciatively of buildings of this period, and when J. J. Stevenson came to extend Christ's College in the 1880s he paid homage to the Fellows' Building by repeating its façade. Since it is quite easy to confuse late nineteenth-century free classical buildings with early seventeenth-century classicism, it is worth walking on to the next court to look at Stevenson's version. The differences are slight, and can mostly be accounted for by a typically Victorian concern for light and air and for economical planning. The dormers sit above the balustrade which is merely decorative and the whole ground floor is raised with ventilation below. The building is thicker than the Fellows' Building and its stone façade is used as a wrap only to the front elevation. Around the back a domestic red-brick style emerges. So, unlike the free-standing Fellows' Building, it has a definite front and back. Internally, where the Fellows' Building has generous broad dog-leg stairs with original crudely carved oak balusters, Stevenson's stairs are tighter and more intricate, with carefully proportioned stone surrounds to the door cases and delightful shallow relieving arches creating frames to the windows and pairs of doors. It is this tightness of planning which means that the stair windows on the front façade light half landings rather than full landings and so are out of alignment with the other windows – a dislocation which Stevenson enjoys. As is so frequently the case, even when an architect is being self-consciously contextual, the aesthetic differences we perceive are inextricably bound up with the society within which the building was conceived.

CLARE COLLEGE

There is no better way in Cambridge to study the evolution of English classical architecture than to make a close inspection of the ranges of Clare College's courtyard (Fig. 13). This is the result of a continuous building programme on the site of what was known as Clare Hall between 1638 and 1715. Despite an interruption of more than twenty-five years during the Civil War, the effect internally is one of harmonious continuity. On the entrance front, because of the late eighteenth-century projection of the chapel (see p. 58), the symmetry and formality is less evident, but the south range, seen from across the lawn at King's, forms a most appropriate foil to the famous chapel.

In order to form this straightforward relationship between the two colleges, an exchange of land between King's and Clare had to take place, whereby Clare ceded land to the south-east in exchange for what is now their garden, with a bridge across the Cam. This was a far from simple affair, since two Bishops, the Archbishop of Canterbury, Lord Holland and the Chancellor of the University were all involved until the king ended the dispute.

Three out of the four sides of the court are three storeys with dormers in the roof. These were originally concealed behind battlements where there are now balustrades. The windows of the earlier ranges also had crossed mullions and casements and in the east range arched heads. The stone mullions were removed so that sash windows could be inserted in the 1760s to match the sashes of the subsequent ranges. These were later replaced inside the court by uniform metal casements so that there has been a homogenisation over the years. Nevertheless, the general effect remains much as it was left at the end of the 75-odd years of construction. The gentle projections and recessions of the stonework on the east range are the means by which the façade retains a vertical rhythm, since the mouldings running between the main three-light windows and the breaking back and forth of the entablature at each level suggest that these projections are almost bay windows. In contrast to the severity of the main range, the gateway has rusticated columns, a semicircular oriel window, and an elaborately decorated top storey with a segmented pediment. This ostentatious vocabulary is partly intended as a display of learning to impress those cultured enough to 'read' the classical style.

The plainness of the south range is accounted for because it carries on the wall pattern of the earlier construction without the interruption of a contrasting sculptured gateway. The river front of the west range exhibits the influence of the more correct and powerful classicism that had begun to appear in Cambridge, particularly that of Christopher Wren, and has a continuous range of Ionic pilasters. These are less peculiar than the extraordinary corner pilasters at Christ's College Fellows' Building (p. 49), but still display a certain amateurishness of detail. (The cills on this front were lowered in the nineteenth century so that the proportion of window to wall is not as originally intended.) Next, the north range, of only two storeys, was constructed using a more pared down and abstracted modelling of the wall-plane and continuous entablature without breaking backwards and forwards as all the other ranges do. Robert Grumbold, the mason for Wren's Trinity Library whose river front has a similar abstract quality, was paid for a drawing in 1683, so that the refinement is the result not just of a developing taste but also of the employment of a knowledgeable mason who had contacts with the world of scholarly architecture. The west range, which had not been completed before the start of the north, was finally finished in 1715, with a two-storey bay surmounted by a segmental pediment, above a round-headed rusticated arch. The character of this last gate seems carefully judged to weld together the themes of the various ranges in the court, where the classical language has been employed with those subtle shifts of syntax and vocabulary which only a close reading will distinguish.

The 1639 bridge, with its robust diagonally set balusters and large decorative balls, was the earliest classical bridge in Cambridge, and is the oldest to survive by Thomas Grumbold. It can be compared instructively with that of 1712 for St John's by Grumbold's son, Robert, working to Wren's outline drawings. The later bridge is more sober, less playful and less likely perhaps to inspire the affection in which the bridge at Clare has been held for many generations. The reflection is prompted as to how far, in architecture, character and correctness are in conflict with each other.

13 Clare College, view of the west range

Notes on further reading

The clearest summary of the principles of classical architecture, to which the introduction to this chapter is indebted, is John Summerson's 1963 radio talks, reprinted many times as *The Classical Language of Architecture*. Also instructive, with numerous plan illustrations, is *Classical Architecture: The Poetics of Order* by Tzonis and Lefaivre. Summerson's essay on Inigo Jones in *The Unromantic Castle and Other Essays* emphasises his view of the latter's importance and originality.

CHAPTER 5

Seventeenth- and eighteenth-century classicism
(1663–1800)

WREN IN CAMBRIDGE

Chapter 4 described how during the sixteenth century the classical language was adopted in Cambridge; this chapter will demonstrate its full flowering, most significantly in one of Christopher Wren's masterpieces, the library at Trinity College. The general pattern of building, however, remained in many respects medieval, a question of Gothic survival, and in at least one celebrated case, Gothic revival. The new language was both 'antique' and 'modern', and when St John's College built their library in the early seventeenth century, as correspondence in the college records indicates, there was a self-conscious decision to follow 'the old fashion of windows', which would be more compatible with the existing fabric. We have already seen something of the survival in the Perpendicular arches on the west front of Peterhouse's chapel, built between 1635 and 1644. Less than twenty years later, in 1663, work began on the chapel at Pembroke College, to the designs of Christopher Wren.

Wren is usually considered Britain's greatest architect, though some would accord that honour to his brilliant pupil Hawksmoor, whose projects for King's College are described below. Until the age of thirty, Wren was engaged in the pursuit of science: as an undergraduate in Oxford he was part of a circle who founded the Royal Society, and he became Gresham Professor of Astronomy in London in 1657 but returned to Oxford as Savilian Professor four years later. Both the cast of his mind (inventive, empirical and quintessentially English) and the reason for his turn to architecture have been carefully analysed by John Summerson. He combined engineering practicality with scholarship and classical learning in a way which is characteristic of the pre-enlightenment mind, making no distinction between what we would call 'science' and 'art'. To Wren, whose thoughts on the subject were recorded by his son in the

Parentalia, there was no question that the correct style of architecture was the antique or classical, and whenever he had the opportunity he aspired to such correctness. Frequently, especially in his religious buildings such as the fifty-one city churches in London and even at St Paul's Cathedral, compromises, demanded by the liturgy or the tastes of his patrons, were forced upon him, but his style is able to embrace and even rejoice in these. At Pembroke, however, the first impression is surely of correctness. To compare the west fronts of the two adjacent college chapels, Peterhouse and Pembroke, is as clear a way as any to see the contrast between an architecture of additive pragmatism and one which embraces a rule-based discipline. The contrast is especially pertinent when we realise that Wren obtained the commission for the work at Pembroke because his uncle, Matthew Wren, Bishop of Ely, had given the £5,000 necessary for its construction in 1659, in fulfilment of a vow he had made when imprisoned in the Tower of London. Matthew Wren, before his imprisonment, had been Master of Peterhouse from 1625 to 1634 and had been responsible for building its chapel. One imagines it was satisfying for him to see his nephew's demonstration of scholarly correctness for Pembroke as a result of his generosity.

Wren refers to the plates of Serlio, not (as Dr Caius did, p. 45) merely for motifs but as a guide to the construction of a sober and dignified street elevation that is characterised by abstract restraint, judiciously relieved by the decoration of the giant Corinthian pilasters and the finely carved garlands in the pediment. The giant pilasters themselves, placed in the proper relationship to each other and the façade as a whole, can be compared to the Ionic pilasters at either end of the Fellows' Building at Christ's (p. 49), used merely as icons of modernity. The a–b–a (narrow, wide, narrow) rhythm of the arches, a motif derived originally from the Roman triumphal arch, does not reflect (as it does in the churches of Alberti or some of the Serlio plates) an aisled church behind but is used symbolically to denote the church triumphant.

Originally the chapel was free standing. Hitcham's Cloisters to the north were added a few years later. The expression is classical towards the court, but medieval towards the street, a telling early indication of the concern for harmony and adjustment to context that remains a characteristic of British architecture.

At Emmanuel College, where he designed the chapel and long gallery, Wren's style is less pure. The pattern is similar to that of Peterhouse, with open arcades adjoining the west end of the chapel. Although the first-floor gallery runs in front of the chapel, the pediment is brought forward to the court elevation and thus represents the chapel on the court façade. The wider central bay creates an awkwardness: either the arches are all the same and the piers on each side of the central columns have to be wider than the other piers, which Wren seems to have intended on his drawings, or else the central archway has to be wider: it is in fact constructed as a curious depressed segmental arch. Trinity College Library, Wren's third and finest building in Cambridge which is

Map 4

Ⓐ Trinity College Library
Ⓑ St Catharine's College
Ⓒ King's College Fellows' Building
Ⓓ Peterhouse Master's Lodge

Other buildings mentioned
① Pembroke College chapel
② Emmanuel College chapel
③ Senate House
④ Clare College chapel
⑤ Emmanuel College Front Court
⑥ 'Little Trinity'
⑦ Malcolm Street
⑧ Park Terrace

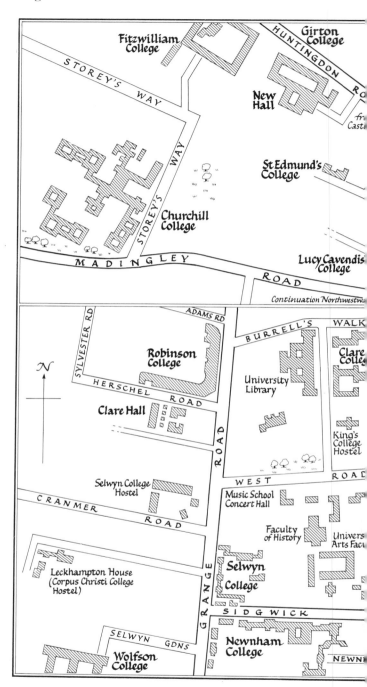

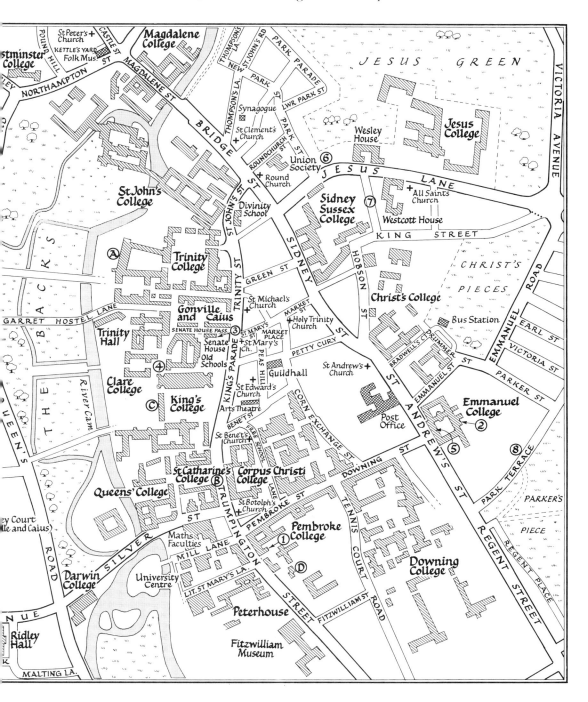

considered in more detail below, has its own idiosyncrasies, but they are more firmly controlled.

By the time Wren died in 1723, his own version of classicism, to say nothing of that of his pupil Hawksmoor's, had fallen from favour and a new stricter manner was fashionable. Wren and Hawksmoor took their inspiration not only from the pattern-books of Serlio but also from the work of contemporary French and Italian architects, such as Bernini, whom Wren met briefly on a visit to Paris in 1665–6. In 1715, with the publication of *Vitruvius Britannicus* by Colin Campbell, and under the patronage of Lord Burlington, a new 'Palladian' taste was proclaimed. As its name implies, this style looked to the Italian architect Palladio (1508–80) for inspiration, though it was very much through the eyes of Inigo Jones, and it is this purer manner which is evident in eighteenth-century buildings in Cambridge by less well-known architects. James Burrough is the principal figure in the early eighteenth century. He was educated at Caius and obtained his MA in 1716. From 1754 to 1765 when he died he was Master of his old college. In the words of Willis and Clark 'his works are not characterised by great artistic power', yet he appears to have collaborated in some capacity with James Gibbs in the design of the Senate House. Much of his work consisted in re-facing and Italianising older buildings, such as the first courts at Trinity Hall and Peterhouse. His new buildings include a range for Peterhouse, fronting Trumpington Street, in pure Palladian style, which was part of a more ambitious scheme, and the chapel at Clare. Although somewhat derivative of Wren's work at Pembroke, this is a tactful and masterly exercise in adding to the college. The ante-chapel is octagonal, with a delightful lantern, and the quality of light and detailing of the interior fittings is superb. James Essex (1722–84) completed part of his work at Clare and continued his idiom into the later eighteenth century with a series of well-mannered buildings such as the combination room for Trinity College, on the west side of Great Court, and the street frontage of Emmanuel College of 1769, a full century after Wren's chapel and long gallery. It has a grand cloister on the east side and an Ionic pediment facing west opposite Downing Street – good mannered rather than powerful or inspired.

These new buildings and re-facings are carried out in stone and this may be an appropriate moment to reflect briefly on the materials of Cambridge architecture. Compared to Oxford or Bath, Cambridge is a city of brick, but Jurassic stone was also used from the earliest times, quarried in what used to be the smallest county of England, Rutland – an area which is still referred to by this name by its inhabitants long after it was swallowed up in Local Government reorganisation. A belt of limestone of variable quality runs through England from the River Humber in the north-east through Lincolnshire, Northamptonshire, the Cotswolds and Gloucestershire to Bath and Somerset. Many of the college buildings in Oxford used stone from Headington, which has proved less durable than stones from Rutland and Northamptonshire: Barnack (used for Fenland priories and abbeys but virtually exhausted by the time of the first considerable expansion of the University, according to Donovan Purcell), Weldon, Clipsham and Ketton. These were transported to Cambridge on barges by river and dike. The most popular was Ketton; it has an even creamy appearance with the occasional pinkish tinge. It was used for most of King's College Chapel, at Clare and for the Fellows' Building at Christ's, by Wren at Pembroke, Emmanuel and Trinity and extensively by Burrough and Essex. Gibbs, as we shall see, used the whitish Portland stone; the quarries at Portland had been expanded because most of Wren's buildings in London used it. In the nineteenth century, Ancaster stone became more available because the advent of the railway made it economic to quarry further afield, though many architects such as Wilkins stuck to Ketton. Continuing repair to churches as well as college buildings ensured that quarries remained open to meet a renewed demand in the later twentieth century by a generation of patrons who were sufficiently disenchanted with the weathering properties of concrete to pay the necessary cost differential.

The eighteenth century is the period when urban domestic architecture flourished in England, and also the time when a series of grand country houses and their gardens were constructed. Examples of both are to be found in Cambridge and nearby. One of the best early eighteenth-century houses, completed in 1701, became the Master's Lodge of Peterhouse in 1727 (see pp. 66–8). Its thick-mullioned windows, near the face of the wall, can be compared to those in the 1725 façade of 'Little Trinity', 16 Jesus Lane, which is representative of the translation of classical principles into a decorous brick architecture. Here the windows are set back in the brick reveals, a pattern which was first adopted in London following the passing of an act in 1709, reinforced in 1774, which required timber to be protected, and later spread to all parts of England and Ireland. The windows themselves have elegant narrow painted mahogany glazing bars. Internally, original panelling survives in a number of rooms, and the gates and piers are especially fine. Cambridge does not have streets or squares of eighteenth-century housing, like London, Bath or Dublin; the urban terraces such as Malcolm Street, or Park Terrace on Parker's Piece, are nineteenth-century, though in a manner which recalls the style fashionable in the capital of some years earlier. The best and most accessible eighteenth-century house is Wimpole Hall, some 10 miles west of Cambridge. Parts of the house date from the seventeenth century. The library, of 1719, is by Gibbs, with a later extension in the 1790s by Soane, but the main front by Flitcroft and the decoration of the entrance hall dates from 1742–5. Here, rather than in any building in the city of Cambridge, it is possible to experience fully the domestic application of the classical style – from the formal and dignified façade, through carefully modulated sequences of interior volume, to the tasteful application of mouldings and decoration.

TRINITY COLLEGE LIBRARY

Wren's third building in Cambridge, and undoubtedly the most important, is the library at Trinity College (Fig. 14). As we have seen, Thomas Nevile, the dynamic Master of Trinity from 1593, had re-fashioned Great Court, combining ranges of earlier buildings to form the largest courtyard in Oxford or Cambridge, had constructed the hall, and begun Trinity's second court which bears his name in the early years of the seventeenth century. On its completion in 1612 it was a shallow U-shape facing the Backs. During and after the construction of Wren's Library its wings were extended, three storeys tall with gabled windows on the top floor and attached pilasters in a Jacobean manner. In 1756 the ubiquitous James Essex, in repairing these poorly constructed ranges, removed the attached pilasters, and replaced the gabled windows by a parapeted third storey.

In 1666, after a fire had destroyed the college's earlier library, Wren was called in by his friend Isaac Barrow, the Master of the college and a fellow member of the Royal Society. His first idea was for a circular free-standing building, an inappropriate geometry for a college library, one might think, but a form which had precedents in Italian Renaissance city plans. The library as constructed also refers to Italian precedent, to Michelangelo's Biblioteca Laurenziana, to Palladio's work at Vicenza and to Sansovino's library in Venice. At the time of its construction it would certainly have been the most foreign-looking building in Cambridge, with, on the Nevile's Court side, a full Ionic order standing above a Tuscan Doric ground-floor arcade. Facing the Backs the orders are omitted and Tuscan gates decorate the plain stone ground floor. The open cloister, preserving the views and the breezes, has a single row of columns in the centre of the arcade. These sit below the central passageway of the library. Structurally it would have been more logical to have had a double row of columns, placed beneath the ends of the bookcases, but this would have cluttered the arcade. The floor had to be strengthened during the building's construction both by additional timbers in its own depth, and by metal rods running diagonally through the pairs of bookcases bolted to the library walls. When the library was repaired in the 1960s further remedial action was taken and there is now steelwork concealed within the floor. The roof trusses, on the other hand, which are softwood, have needed little attention and the structure over the north staircase (an identical south stair was planned but not executed), which is geometrically complex and exceedingly thin in section, has never even been exposed.

Viewed from Nevile's Court the entablature at first-floor level lines with the second-floor parapet of the rest of the court. But while the classical grammar is obeyed, and a proper proportion between the two orders established, the floor level of the library is in

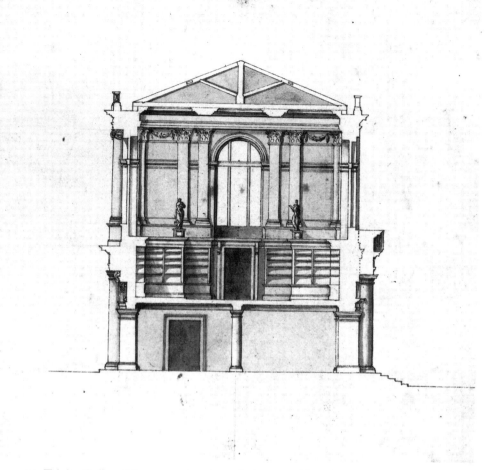

14 Trinity College Library: section through the central bay shown in a drawing by Wren, with Nevile's Court to the left and the Backs to the right

fact at the bottom of the ground-floor arches, which are filled with sculpted panels, and thus matches the floor levels of the adjacent buildings. 'By this contrivance', as Wren wrote to a member of the college, 'the windows of the library rise high and give place for desks against the walls', and not only desks, for, as can be seen in the section (Fig. 14), the large arched windows are comfortably above the bookcases which run against the walls as well as projecting to form thirty U-shaped book-lined bays.

The four statues represent Divinity (shrouded and holding a book), Law (with a scroll), Physics (with a staff and serpent) and Mathematics (who counts on her fingers). As Wren explained, this is the only stress the centre needs:

I have given noe other Frontispiece to the middle than the statues, according to ancient example, because in this case I find anything else to be impertinent, the entrances being endwise, and the roofe not suiting it.

We know, from a letter of Wren's preserved at All Souls, Oxford, that he took particular care about the interior detail: 'We are scrupulous in small matters, and you must pardon us; the Architects are as great pedants as Criticks or Heralds.' Wren designed not only the bookcases but also the tables and chairs, and provided full-size profiles of the various mouldings. As the section indicates, he originally intended statues on the ends of the cedar bookcases rather than the present busts. Some of these and all the crests and coats of arms, carved from laminated sheets of limewood with luxuriant vegetation, animals and insects, are by Grinling Gibbons and ensure that the detail of the interior is as sumptuous as the general arrangement is ingenious.

This brilliant solution to the problem of inserting a monumental new building into the domestically scaled court, with tact as well as boldness, by the exercise of an unusual 'contrivance' in the manipulation of the classical language and mathematical skill in the design of the structure, represents Wren's, and more generally British architecture at its inventive best.

ST CATHARINE'S COLLEGE – PRINCIPAL COURT

Although St Catharine's was founded in 1473, the earliest visible buildings date from the seventeenth century and begin an apparently well-matched open court facing east on to Trumpington Street (Fig. 15). Where Gibbs, Wren and Hawksmoor are architects of international stature, the designers of the principal court at St Catharine's have only a local notoriety: they appear to have been a Mr Elder, perhaps the same Elder who was a bricklayer for one of Wren's city churches in 1689, and Robert Grumbold, who was to complete the court at Clare (p. 51) and who was Wren's mason at Trinity Library. Building work took place between 1674 and 1704 in a consistent brick manner. The college does not reflect the most recent architectural fashion so much as accommodate the classical manner to the college pattern which had become so established by then. We know from Loggan's print of 1688 that the east end was intended to be closed by a two-storeyed range with a library and gatehouse. The main entrance was from the west, off Queens' Lane, and the gateway is emphasised by its stone cladding, its attached Tuscan columns on the ground floor and two-storey Ionic pilasters (Corinthian columns on the court side) above. The crowning segmental (that is to say fatter than semicircular) pediment is broken in the centre, a favourite device of seventeenth-century Baroque architects. Inside the court the doorways to the staircases on the west face break through the thickened base and are decorated with stone quoins.

15 St Catharine's College

The windows are stone with a central mullion, and have metal casements, not the sliding sash windows that were invented apparently simultaneously in England, Scotland and Holland and were to become such an essential component of the Georgian style. Even though none of it is now visible, the Royal Commission on Historical Monuments suggests that the incorporation of older fabric accounts for the different floor levels of the west range and the larger-scaled north and south ranges. The asymmetry of the site ensures that the court itself is irregular: the south range is several bays larger than the north. The result is a collision in the south-west corner of the court – something which is acceptable and enjoyable in buildings of the past but which architects have usually striven to avoid, or occasionally striven to contrive.

The college suffered financial problems, which meant an appeal had to be launched in 1698 after the death of Eachard, the Master, who had been principally responsible for the programme of works over a period of some twenty-four years. The appeal was successful so that the college managed to continue building the chapel and the range of rooms opposite which were completed only in the 1770s. Here both Burrough and Essex were involved but confined themselves to imitating the pattern already established. In the nineteenth century the windows to the hall and library were Gothicised and the projecting oriel window added, and in the twentieth century (1930

63

and 1949) Kennedy and Nightingale made nearly symmetrical additions right up to Trumpington Street, further enlarging the court, and continuing the early eighteenth-century Baroque manner of the existing buildings.

The result is an ensemble that at first sight is merely consistent, conservative and well mannered but which repays close examination. For every slight variation tells its story, of patient adaptation of original models by architects and masons who aspired to make a decent whole rather than to attempt a masterpiece.

KING'S COLLEGE FELLOWS' BUILDING

King's College used to occupy a site to the north of the famous chapel, and its gatehouse is still visible as part of the west range of what is now the Old Schools. The present arrangement of the college, lying to the south of the chapel, was envisaged by Henry VI in his 'Will' of 1448, but it was only in the 1690s that King's began to build along King's Parade (in an area now replaced by Wilkins' screen) and not until 1713 did the Provost meet Christopher Wren (by then aged 80) to talk over plans. They met in his pupil Nicholas Hawksmoor's home in Kensington and discussed a grandiose Baroque scheme for a court nearly 90 metres square. Models of Hawksmoor's proposal (for he was certainly the principal designer) survive and show buildings of unparalleled sculptural power in Cambridge – one of them with a giant order of columns and the second with giant pilasters flattened against the wall-plane. It is uncertain whether these are alternative versions of the Fellows' Building, since John Adams, the Provost, records his preference for pilasters as a 'plainer manner', or, as Willis and Clark think, models of the east and west ranges. The arrangement of the rooms was volumetrically inventive since pairs of study bedrooms are stacked above each other giving on to a shared sitting room of double the bedroom's height, a pattern that both refers to the precedent of medieval college arrangements and anticipates the twentieth-century experiments of Le Corbusier in his Unités d'Habitation. The U-shaped plan, cloistered on three sides, is carefully dimensioned to relate to the spacing of the buttresses of the chapel so that the whole courtyard would have had a powerful coherence.

A tantalising sketch survives in the British Museum from Hawksmoor's hand in which he seems to suggest a complete re-ordering of the city of Cambridge on similarly striking Roman lines: amongst other improvements, Trinity Street would have contained a pair of obelisks like the Piazza Navona, and a grand square with an arcaded screen would have been formed relating King's College Chapel, Great St Mary's and new university buildings. But England has seldom supported such vision; both natural cautiousness and the absence of a single source of power, particularly in a town as politically complex as Cambridge, prevent the fulfilment of the grand plans that were achieved in Italy and France. As Vanbrugh, his fellow architect at Blenheim Palace,

16 King's College Fellows' Building, adjacent to the famous chapel

remarked on Hawksmoor's death, 'What would Monsieur Colbert have done with such a man?'

Adams failed to raise the necessary money for Hawksmoor's buildings before he died in 1719 and by 1723 we find the college paying James Gibbs for drawings. Gibbs, who was born in Aberdeen, had studied under Carlo Fontana in Rome and his first buildings in England reflect Italian influence. He replaced Hawksmoor both at King's and at Oxford, with his Radcliffe Camera, and developed an individual style which is neither as restrained as the English Palladians nor as powerful and sculpturally over-whelming as Hawksmoor at his most majestic. Historically he is one of Britain's most influential architects because his *Book of Architecture* of 1728 publicised his designs in Europe and in America where his St Martin-in-the-Fields, with its conjunction of temple front and spire, set the pattern for innumerable painted clapboard churches.

Gibbs' Fellows' Building (Fig. 16), part of an unrealised scheme for a complete court composed of three free-standing buildings, is in the same position and alignment as Hawksmoor had planned his own. It has no cloister and is set a deferential distance from the chapel, which we know from his book Gibbs admired. Its façade progression from rusticated base to 'piano nobile' and balustraded upper floor is well mannered and relatively plain, but with a strongly emphasised central semicircular window, invaded by enough of the pediment below to impart some tension to the composition. Reclining figures were intended on the pediment which would have further enriched the effect. The building retains the distinction between court-facing and 'Backs'-facing façades, which Hawksmoor's scheme had dramatised, in a subtle way. The 'urban' east front towards the court has twenty-one bays and hence a narrower stretch of wall between each window than the seventeen-bayed west front which appears much calmer. The building is entirely clad in white Portland stone in contrast to the chapel's warm yellow Ketton and York stone; of course it is wholly classical rather than Gothic. Despite its large chimneys, Gibbs' building is predominantly horizontal in feeling: because of the concealed valley gutter and low-pitched roofs the regular balustrade of the Gibbs building appears against the skyline compared with the frequent vertical punctuations of the chapel's pinnacles (of which Ruskin so disapproved that he described it as 'like a sow on its back'). The contrast between the two is extreme: each is a faithful expression of its time and Gibbs makes no concessions to the manner or material of the masterpiece he adjoins. Yet this pair of buildings, seen from across the Backs, forms one of the most admired and most frequently photographed architectural compositions in the town – a clear example that 'keeping in keeping' is not always the right recipe for success. The change of taste, discussed in chapter 6, between 1714 and 1823, when William Wilkins built the hall range to the south and the famous screen, can be illustrated by Wilkins' proposal to 'Gothicise' Gibbs' Fellows' Building so that it should conform with the rest of the court. Thankfully, this never happened.

Gibbs was also the architect for the University's Senate House just down King's Parade, again in Portland stone, which elegantly resolves the complex requirements of the University's liturgy by giving equal emphasis to the east-facing gable and the pedimented central bay on the south side. The fine interior woodwork is by James Essex, father and son. Gibbs had intended a three-sided court on to King's Parade but the third side was never built, apparently because Dr Gooch, Master of Caius, complained that it would obscure his view of King's College Chapel, and the block which faces the Senate House lawn was completed by Stephen Wright in a Palladian manner, more English and reticent even than Gibbs.

THE MASTER'S LODGE, PETERHOUSE

This free-standing building, opposite Peterhouse, was built as a private house by one of the Fellows, Dr Charles Beaumont, in 1702 and left to Peterhouse on his death in 1727. There have been some small single-storey additions, but otherwise the house remains as originally built, a grand symmetrical three-storeyed building with a basement. It has a

17 Detail of the staircase balustrade at the Master's Lodge, Peterhouse

low-pitched hipped roof and its plan derives from what was known in the seventeenth century as a 'double pile' house. This means that the hallway, which contains the main staircase and the servants' stairs, runs transversely across the centre of the house, leaving wide-frontage rooms facing east and west. A slight indent on the plan expresses the cross hall, and this can be seen on the south façade. The cornice continues right around the building, emphasising its four-square solidity; the base is of stone and stone quoins are used at the corners. The kitchen was in the north-east corner; its floor was originally at basement level but it was lit and ventilated through ground-floor windows. There are seven bays, and the windows are of different heights on each floor – nine pane on the second floor, fifteen pane on the first floor or 'piano nobile', and twelve pane on the ground floor. The window pattern reflects the use of the house: servants' bedrooms at the top, the main living spaces and principal bedroom on the first floor, entertaining on the ground floor where the butler and housekeeper also lived. As in much Georgian architecture it also reveals the social hierarchy of the occupants. It is because of the connection between a style and the society that produced it that stylistic imitation often seems so weak. Just to the south of the Master's Lodge is a hostel of 1926 by T. H. Lyon, the start of a never-completed new court for Peterhouse. To quote Nikolaus Pevsner, 'it is in an inoffensive neo-Georgian style, and might be a post office'. Here, differences of window proportion are merely visual ordering devices because the bed–sitting rooms are identical floor by floor. Yet the vertical hierarchy of the Master's Lodge can also be seen to reflect another sequence from heavy and earthbound towards the sky and this is an order which is perennial.

Inside the Master's Lodge, most of the panelling is original and the main staircase is especially impressive (Fig. 17). It has three twisted balusters to each step and two clusters of four balusters at the half landing. It was constructed a few years earlier and is more unsophisticated than Dr Bentley's staircase in Trinity's Master's Lodge and that at the Master's Lodge of Clare College, which has miniature Corinthian columns as newel posts. These decorative elements, newel posts, dado rails, door architraves and skirtings are diminutive exercises in classical detail, since the language can be exercised at any scale. If Dr Caius' Gate of Honour reminds us of a mantelpiece clock, some of the best eighteenth-century joinery, in its intricate ordering and sensitivity of proportion, can recall the façades of whole buildings.

Notes on further reading

In addition to the voluminous publications of the Wren Society, there are numerous studies of Wren: Margaret Whinney (1971) may be the most accessible. The *Parentalia* by his son Christopher is a fascinating account of his life and thought. A provocative essay, *The Mind of Wren* was written by John Summerson many years ago and reprinted in his *Heavenly Mansions* of 1949. Hawksmoor's tantalising sketch is discussed in *A Town Plan for Cambridge in the eighteenth century,* one of a set of essays in Frances Keynes' *By-ways of Cambridge History*, and more fully in *The Town of Cambridge as it ought to be Reformed*, privately published by Brooke Crutchley for Cambridge University Press, with a text by David Roberts, illustrated by Gordon Cullen. An excellent short account of the various stones used in Cambridge buildings is Donovan Purcell's *Cambridge Stone*.

Dan Cruickshank's *London: The Art of Georgian Building* gives a clearly illustrated account of the Georgian town house. The complex origins of the sash window are identified in an article of 1983 by H. J. Louw in *Architectural History*.

CHAPTER 6

Nineteenth-century revivalism (1800–1875)

SCHOLARSHIP AND ROMANCE

The mid-eighteenth century marks an important cultural turning point in European history. Whether we speak of the age of enlightenment, the origins of Romanticism or the beginning of the neo-classical movement, it seems that a distinction is made, for the first time, between the rational and the emotional, the objective and the subjective. In architecture, style, previously concerned with correctness, 'modernity' and appeals to antique precedent, is seen as a means of creating literary association. In Britain the novels of Sir Walter Scott are often cited as evidence for the romantic idea that buildings might affect the emotions by association, and some of the earliest neo-Gothic buildings are garden structures, set in a landscape that itself might be designed with an associational literary programme. At Wimpole Hall, mentioned in the last chapter, Sanderson Miller designed a sham ruin in 1749 as a picturesque object to be seen from the house. It would be a goal for summer picnics so that its actual use might be frivolous, but the associational aim became a serious one. One of the most influential Gothic pattern-books, Batty Langley's *Gothic Architecture improved by Rules and Proportions*, had been published two years earlier. The late eighteenth century also saw the increasing popularity and importance of the Grand Tour. Robert Adam, probably the greatest British architect of that period, spent four years abroad from 1754 studying Roman architecture, though he also visited Spalato (or Split). Unfortunately, his grandiose scheme for a University Library in Cambridge, made in 1784, was never executed, and the first architect to bring his studies abroad to fruition was William Wilkins at Downing College (see pp. 75–7).

Wilkins, who lived and died in Cambridge and was the designer of, amongst other buildings, the National Gallery in London, illustrates the eclectic nature of early nineteenth-century taste. His earliest research had been into East Anglian Gothic, before

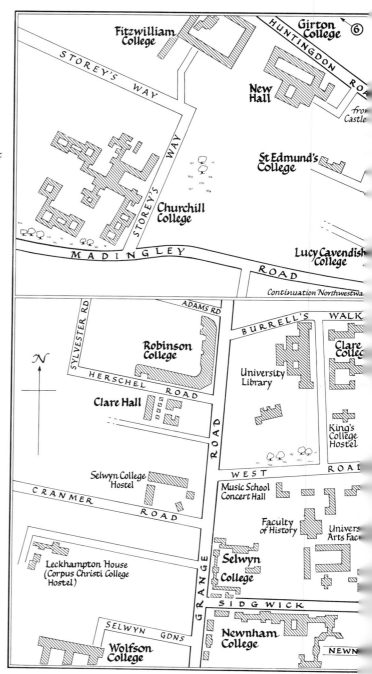

Map 5

(A) Downing College
(B) Old University Library
(C) Pembroke College
(D) All Saints' Church

Other buildings mentioned
(1) Corpus Christi College First Court
(2) King's College screen
(3) St John's College New Court
(4) Fitzwilliam Museum
(5) Jesus College chapel
(6) Girton College
(7) Gonville and Caius College Tree Court
(8) Lloyds Bank

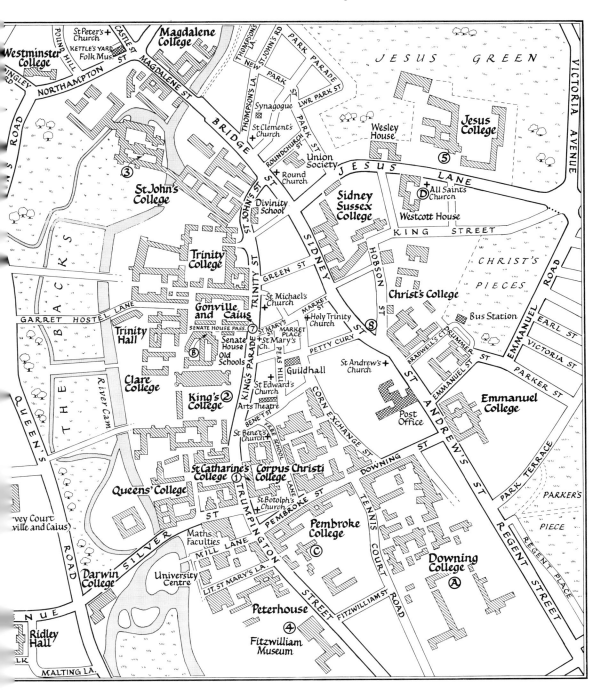

visiting Greece and Asia Minor on a scholarship, and after the Greek-style Downing, he built in the Gothic style for Corpus Christi and Trinity; and for King's the justly famous screen, which is frequently confused with medieval work. Wilkins had measured King's Chapel as an undergraduate and the screen is composed of exactly copied fragments, while the gate can be seen as a miniature version of Wren's Tom Tower at Christ Church, Oxford.

The combination of architectural correctness, as a result of research, and Romantic associationalism is also revealed in Cambridge in the work of Thomas Rickman (1776–1841). Between 1801 and 1803 he had practised medicine, and then went into business and insurance, only setting up as an architect in Liverpool in 1817. He began his study of churches in 1809 and in the year he initiated his practice he published *An attempt to discriminate the styles of architecture in England*, which introduced the terms Early English, Decorated and Perpendicular to distinguish three phases of Gothic architecture (see p. 24). With Henry Hutchinson he was the architect of the New Court at St John's College, built between 1825 and 1831, when the picturesque Bridge of Sighs connecting the court back to the rest of the college was completed. If the bridge and the pinnacled skyline is a romantic Venetian conception, the planning of New Court, which was, at the time, the largest single building erected by a college and faces on to the Backs with a cloistered walk in front, is reminiscent in its general massing of a Palladian country house; its Gothic dress appears rather papery and thin. The effect of stage scenery is enhanced by the institutional brickwork of the rear of the building.

In 1834 Rickman participated in a competition for the design of the Fitzwilliam Museum. In the event this was won by George Basevi – though it had to be completed by Cockerell because of Basevi's untimely death in 1845, when, as surveyor to the cathedral at Ely, he fell through the floor of the belfry of the western tower with fatal consequences. Rickman presented three designs. One was in Gothic mode, like a version of Wyatt's Fonthill Abbey for the eccentric and wealthy connoisseur William Beckford. The perspectives show hugely tall galleries internally and a cathedral-like exterior with gowned figures in the foreground: the reference is obviously to the medieval origins of the university. The second design was in an inflated Roman manner, perhaps because Rome had been the domicile of Viscount Fitzwilliam, who had died in 1815 leaving £100,000 in New South Sea Annuities to the University in order to build the museum which bears his name. Rickman's third design was Greek, with a free-standing colonnade, presumably because many of Fitzwilliam's artefacts, collected during his Roman sojourn, were Greek vases, coins and casts from ancient statues. These three entries, from the hand of a single architect, illustrate the stylistic problem when association becomes the principal driving force: any of the manners is theoretically justifiable. None of Rickman's designs was as distinguished as Basevi's, but this had less to do with their style than the skill of the architects concerned. The

Fitzwilliam has been extended a number of times, but the central building is magnificent: neo-classical vocabulary used to Baroque scenic effect. The major painting galleries are equal to anything of the period abroad, though the richly decorated staircase hall is awkwardly cramped.

GOTHIC PRINCIPLES

Faced with the problem of what manner should be adopted, architects needed some firmer justification for their choice. A. W. N. Pugin, best known for his part in the design of the Houses of Parliament, provided a moral argument for the Gothic style. He had converted to Catholicism in 1834 and in *Contrasts* of 1836 and *The True Principles of Pointed or Christian Architecture* of 1841 argued that it was the 'decay of faith' which had led people to adopt 'the luxurious styles of ancient Paganism'. 'The two great rules for design are these', he wrote in *True Principles*, 'first there should be no features about a building which are not necessary for convenience, construction or propriety; second that all ornament should consist of enrichment of the essential construction of the building'. There were compelling grounds of truthfulness (to the nature of materials, the climate of the British Isles and the character of its inhabitants) for the adoption of a late thirteenth- or early fourteenth-century style. Pugin's own work can be seen at Jesus College, where he extended the choir, removing the late Perpendicular roof with its flat plaster ceiling in favour of a tall pitched roof and 'Early English' lancet windows: the stalls, screen, lectern and floor tiling are also Pugin's.

One effect of Pugin's philosophy, which passed into the writings of Ruskin and historians of the twentieth century, will be referred to later (p. 105). A more immediate influence can be traced through the Ecclesiological or Cambridge Camden Society founded by a group of enthusiasts within the University in May 1839 for the study of 'ecclesiastical antiquities'. The powerful committee of the society determined policy and published *The Ecclesiologist* from 1841 to 1868, as well as a series of tracts and handbooks to reform church liturgy and architecture. Architects were to 'take a religious view of their profession' and very few indeed were approved of. Ambrose Poynter's 1841 St Paul's Church on Hills Road, Cambridge, was severely criticised in the first issue, because its 'style of architecture and plan of internal arrangement should have been after some approved ancient model'. A church by C. R. Cockerell (see below), St Bartholomew's, Moor Lane, London (a rebuilding of a church by Wren), was denounced as 'disgraceful to the age and city in which it is built'. The favoured style was 'Decorated' (in Rickman's terms, even if Rickman, who was a Quaker, was not thoroughly approved of), that originally employed between 1290 and 1350. King's College chapel (which is of course 'Perpendicular') was accused of 'violating that great principal of gothic architecture, vertical ascendancy'. The effect of the Cambridge

Camden Society's dogma on new church building and on the internal arrangements of existing churches was considerable, not only in England but also abroad. In this country it prompted the confident replacement of ancient non-conforming fabric by new in the approved manner by unskilled architects, and the demolishing of fifteenth-century work by skilled ones such as Anthony Salvin who restored the Round Church (Holy Sepulchre: see p. 12).

The problem of 'restoration' was most memorably articulated by William Morris in his 1877 Manifesto of the Society for the Protection of Ancient Buildings (SPAB) and it is perhaps worth examining the position he outlined. He claims that the nineteenth century simultaneously discovered the styles of the past whilst failing to develop a style of its own:

> From this lack and this gain arose in men's minds the strange idea of the Restoration of ancient buildings; and a strange and most fatal idea, which by its very name implies that it is possible to strip from a building this, that, and the other part of its history – of its life that is – and then to stay the hand at some arbitrary point, and leave it still historical, living, and even as it once was.
>
> In early times this kind of forgery was impossible, because knowledge failed the builders, or perhaps instinct held them back. If repairs were needed, if ambition or piety pricked on to change, that change was of necessity wrought in the unmistakable fashion of the time; a church of the eleventh century might be added to or altered in the twelfth, thirteenth, fourteenth, fifteenth, sixteenth, or even the seventeenth or eighteenth centuries; but every change, whatever history it destroyed, left history in the gap, and was alive with the spirit of the deeds done midst its fashioning. The result of all this was often a building in which the many changes, though harsh and visible enough, were, by their very contrast, interesting and instructive and could not possibly mislead. But those who make the changes wrought in our day under the name of Restoration, while professing to bring back a building to the best time of its history, have no guide but each his own individual whim to point out to them what is admirable and what contemptible; while the very nature of their tasks compels them to destroy something and to supply the gap by imagining what the earlier builders should or might have done. Moreover, in the course of this double process of destruction and addition the whole surface of the building is necessarily tampered with; so that the appearance of antiquity is taken away from such old parts of the fabric as are left, and there is no laying to rest in the spectator the suspicion of what may have been lost; and in short, a feeble and lifeless forgery is the final result of all the wasted labour.

Morris' call for 'protection' rather than 'restoration' entails, ideally, leaving buildings exactly as they are and constructing new ones in their stead when changed uses require it. But if alterations and additions are to be made to existing buildings (which is the case with nearly all the Cambridge colleges) he implies that they should be done in the manner of the time rather than as a 'feeble and lifeless forgery'.

DOWNING COLLEGE

To walk into the court at Downing College is to experience a different kind of space from that in other courts in Cambridge, and this is a correct reflection of its designer's conception, even though what we see now falls far short of what was originally envisaged, and the whole arrangement of the buildings, which form a south-facing three-sided court, is the reverse of Wilkins' original intention.

Downing was the first new college to be founded in Cambridge since Sidney Sussex in 1594. Numbers of undergraduates in Cambridge increased dramatically in the early nineteenth century, and the foundation of Downing might be seen as a way of coping with the increase. In fact, Downing owes its origin to the unconsummated marriage of Sir George Downing and the fact that his cousin, Sir Jacob, and indeed all his male relatives who might have inherited his fortune, died childless. Lady Margaret Downing, widow of Sir Jacob, contested the provisions of Sir George's will of 1717, that his properties should go to five trustees who should purchase land and create a new college in Cambridge: all five trustees had died before her husband in 1764. In 1769 the Lord Chancellor declared that the trust Sir George Downing had sought to establish was valid. Lady Margaret's nephew, Jacob Whittington, continued to obstruct the foundation of the college, but finally a Royal Charter was granted in 1800 and statutes published in 1805, nearly ninety years after Sir George Downing conceived the idea.

Early architectural schemes for the new college had been provided by James Essex and after his death by James Wyatt who had already built for several colleges in Oxford as well as Cambridge. The present site was not yet fixed and Wyatt favoured a location on the Backs. Perspective drawings of his scheme survive: a large enclosed square court, rather dull and columned all around the interior in Roman Doric. In 1804, when the site, known as Pembroke Leys, was purchased and Wyatt had presented a set of estimates, the first Master, Francis Annesley, who had been instrumental in resolving the complex litigation which nearly prevented the foundation of the college, took the unusual step of asking the opinion of Thomas Hope about Wyatt's designs. The 35-year-old Hope, later to become one of the most influential critics of the day, had returned in 1795 from an eight-year Grand Tour, enthused with the purity of Greek art. He published as a pamphlet his letter to the Master of Downing concerning the design of the college, thus using the opportunity to create a polemical statement on behalf of the Graecophils – a loose affiliation of Cambridge scholars, which included Lord Byron, who were passionate about all things Greek. Greek architecture answered the new taste for external sobriety and plainness and for archaeological correctness. Renaissance interpretations of the classical language from the sixteenth century onwards were seen as compromised and tired. Everything about Wyatt's elevations, wrote Hope, 'is trite, commonplace, nay, often vulgar'. (These were brave words: Wyatt was President of the Royal Academy at the time, and Hope was excluded from the Academy dinner in 1804 because of the furore he caused.) Hope recommended William Wilkins, whose family were East Anglian builders but who was at that time a mathematician with an interest in architectural antiquities. He had returned in 1804 to a fellowship at his old college, Gonville and Caius, after his own three-year Grand Tour. The college considered the original Wyatt scheme, and alternatives by George Byfield, Francis Sandys, Lewis Wyatt (nephew of James) and Wilkins himself. William Porden also submitted an elaborate Gothic scheme. The final choice (between Wilkins and Lewis Wyatt) was made with the help of three London architects, who despite a number of reservations (such as 'the winding subterranean passage of 140 feet in length' connecting the kitchen and hall) preferred Wilkins' scheme unanimously, provided that he could satisfy them with a revised plan, which he did by June 1806. With the exception of Porden, each of the architects had reacted to Hope's criticism of the original Wyatt scheme.

Wilkins' revolutionary perception was that a Greek design would consist of a number of separate pavilions, which in their grouping would suggest a court, rather than the application of Greek-derived decoration to a Renaissance or Palladian plan. It was this which caused the problematic connection between kitchen and dining room, noted by the London architects. In the revised scheme parallel north and south ranges are created consisting of rooms (or 'apartments'), with a central detached house for a professor (Law on the east side, 'Physic' or medicine on the west). Turning the corner are the Master's Lodge (east) (Fig. 18) and the hall (west), both of which have pediments on two sides. Across the southern end was to have been a monumental temple-like building, with porticoes at the east and west ends and an engaged order on north and south. This contained the library and college chapel back-to-back. The college was approached from the north, through a gateway building or propylaea. It has frequently been pointed out how Wilkins' campus plan anticipates by at least ten years that of Thomas Jefferson at the University of Virginia. But neither the south buildings nor the propylaea, which were to be in the severest Greek Doric, was built, and in the twentieth century Sir Herbert Baker, followed by his partner Alex Scott, closed the north end with a three-storey range of rooms and a central chapel, suggesting a strong east–west axis with an imposing gate to Regent Street. This too was never constructed. Furthermore, what Wilkins intended as plain screen walls separating the north–south ranges of rooms and the houses have been filled in with rooms, so that the appearance today is of a more continuous wall of building. The fact that the ranges were not meant to be understood in this way can be perceived most obviously by the different head heights of the first-floor windows of the 'houses' (particularly that in the east range) and the 'apartments'.

18 Downing College: the Master's Lodge at the southern end of the east range

There was an undeniable awkwardness, indeed amateurishness, to certain aspects of the planning of this, Wilkins' first building. Internal spaces are sandwiched together to achieve the necessary external expression. Yet, as the magnificent set of drawings retained by the college attests, every profile of the restrained Greek Ionic order was minutely considered. The remarkably plain, unadorned ranges are contrasted with the more elaborate hall and lodge, and the sought-for illusion, of temple structures in an undisturbed landscape, can still make a powerful effect, particularly framing the diagonal view of the 1890 Catholic Church. It is worth examining the Ionic capitals of the Master's Lodge and hall: they turn the corner in two different ways, both sanctioned by antique precedent.

There is a 1964 combination room by Howell next to the hall, abstracted, confident, if a trifle mannered, but a successful building of its own time which, by the use of a plain screen wall and the continuation of Wilkins' elevated plinth, or stylobate, respects the nineteenth-century work. It can be compared with a series of buildings of the 1980s and 1990s by Quinlan Terry, some in a most un-Greek classical style employing, in the case of the Howard Building, each of the orders, rustications, Baroque doorcases and oval windows which would have been heavily criticised by Thomas Hope and the Graecophils.

THE OLD UNIVERSITY LIBRARY

C. R. Cockerell was a very different architect from William Wilkins. He was no less of a scholar or antiquarian. On his Grand Tour between 1810 and 1817, he had been the first to observe the entasis (slight swelling) on the columns of the Parthenon, though characteristically, unlike the opportunistic Wilkins who published his *Magna Graecia* in 1807 within three years of his return from Greece, he failed to publish the results of his own research (*The Temples of Jupiter Panhellenius at Aegina, and of Apollo Epicurius at Bassae*) until 1860 when the Greek revival was far from fashionable. On Wilkins' death in 1839 Cockerell was appointed to the Professorship of Architecture he had vacated at the Royal Academy and lectured to appreciative audiences from 1841 to 1856. He was a sensitive but ruthless critic. Of Wilkins' Downing he noted tersely in 1822, 'Quadrangle too wide, buildings too sunk, like a string of sausages', and of his neo-Gothic work at King's he wrote, 'the whole system is conceived in a servile spirit of imitation'. Yet he admired the same architect's house at The Grange, Hampshire, to which he himself made additions. Already, on his Grand Tour, his diaries betray a sympathy for Roman architecture as much as Greek, and his Academy lectures as well as his own buildings reveal the influence of Palladio, Alberti and even the Baroque architects Bernini and Borromini. Amongst English architects he particularly admired Wren, Vanbrugh and Hawksmoor and for the benefit of his students he prepared in 1838 a 'tribute to the memory of Christopher Wren' in the form of a painting depicting all of Wren's most famous buildings, crowned by St Paul's. He was sceptical of the Greek revival as a fashion ('that vicious mode of composition of lapping under and over') seeking a more complex synthesis of the best classical precedents.

Cockerell's scholarly sensitivity was perhaps incompatible with the ambitious and entrepreneurial character required to ensure a string of lucrative commissions, but he was a respected figure and was frequently invited to participate in competitions: in these he was seldom successful outright, and though the commission for the new University Library did eventually fall to him, it was not without its complications. He was invited to send in designs by the University's Vice-Chancellor in the summer of 1829, in competition with Decimus Burton, Rickman and Hutchinson (see p. 72) and William Wilkins. No cost limits had been set for meeting the brief which was for museums, lecture rooms and offices as well as the library itself. On 25 November his scheme was chosen, but the University was now nervous of the costs involved. A second competition, on a reduced site and to a maximum budget of £25,000, was held and this time the submission by Rickman and Hutchinson was preferred. After three more years of political in-fighting a further competition between the same three firms, for the library only, was won conclusively by Cockerell in May 1836. Research by twentieth-

19 The Old University Library, north-west corner

century scholars has helped us to understand the evolution of Cockerell's design. The grand earlier schemes would have created a monumental courtyard replacing the Old Schools and the adjacent court which had been purchased by the University from King's College in 1829 when Wilkins had completed their new ranges. Gibbs and before him Hawksmoor and Wren had envisaged a new court, of which the Senate House would form a relatively minor part of the composition, and Robert Adam had prepared a similar scheme in 1784. The present library is only the equivalent of the north wing of Cockerell's proposal, in the centre of which facing the lawn, where Wright's delicate arcade now stands, would have been a Corinthian portico, containing paired external staircases rather like Schinkel's 1823 Altes Museum in Berlin. At either side were austere Greek Doric stoae, open cloisters, the northern one of which would have linked with Gibbs' Senate House.

Even as a fragment, the library is impressive enough. It achieves its effect by Cockerell's choice of architectural forms, his use of material and sculpting of the wall-plane and, in the interior, his masterly handling of volume and surface. The east façade is an exercise in the triumphal arch motif (see p. 55). A severe Doric entablature, resting on plain pilasters is dramatically split by a great arch which invades the rusticated attic. The arch introduces a major theme of the building: the seven transverse barrel vaults over the reading bays shedding a beautiful even light to the long east–west vault of the main room. The arcade down the north façade, along Senate House Passage, encloses the lunettes lighting these transverse vaults and frames the upper-storey windows. The windows on the lower level are contained within a sub-frame, so that the principal wall-plane is completely undecorated, and this prepares us for the astonishing plain and sculptural north-west corner, where Cockerell turns the awkward angle of the site to magnificent architectural effect (Fig. 19). The rusticated base is formed of massive stones, something that Cockerell was particularly fond of. As Watkin says, 'no one who passes down Senate House passage can fail to be moved by the austerity and magnitude of this façade'.

The vault of the library is brickwork, for fireproofing, plastered with a bold diagonal pattern which seems inspired by Roman Baroque precedents. Paired Ionic columns herald the entrance to the room, and these are derived from the temple of Apollo at Bassae which Cockerell had studied so closely. Even though it is only a part of a much grander conception, the library is still Cambridge's finest nineteenth-century building – the impossibility of pigeon-holing its scholarly architect stylistically is an indication of its originality; its power to move us today testifies to its enduring architectural quality.

When Scott's University Library (p. 95) was constructed in 1934, Cockerell's building became the Seeley History Library and after the construction of the new History Faculty in 1968 (p. 108), the Squire Law Library. When the Squire, in turn, moves to the Sidgwick site, the building will go to Caius College: a more splendid college library can hardly be imagined.

PEMBROKE COLLEGE

Alfred Waterhouse (1830–1905) ran one of the most successful architectural practices in the country between 1865 and the end of the century. He had begun in Manchester in 1856, where he built the Assize Court and the Town Hall, both Gothic in expression, but with exceedingly clear plans. His unsuccessful competition entry for the Law Courts in the Strand in London of 1866 was a masterpiece of the complex

20 The Red Building, Pembroke College

interweaving of the different strands of the brief. His buildings are often faced in hard red brick, as at Girton or Pump Court in Jesus College, or in terracotta (clay that has been fired in a mould), for the headquarters of the Prudential Assurance Building in London or the Natural History Museum where pink and blue terracotta alternate. At Gonville and Caius he rebuilt Tree Court in 1870 in a stone-faced French early Renaissance style with a large tower on to King's Parade. His self-confident assertiveness, evident at Caius where his building completely changed the scale of this part of the town, is easy to criticise, but his technical competence is never in doubt.

At Pembroke, Waterhouse replaced a row of houses on Trumpington Street with what is known for obvious reasons as the Red Building (Fig. 20) and at the same time built a new Master's Lodge in 1871–2. In 1874 he was commissioned to prepare plans for an extension to the hall and the erection of a new combination room. The old hall was found to be in such a poor state that Waterhouse's advice was followed and it was demolished despite the protests of several members of the fellowship. It was this propensity to demolish and rebuild, or radically to restore old buildings, by architects in the nineteenth century (such as George Gilbert Scott Senior, the architect for St John's College Chapel in 1863, which replaced the former chapel and infirmary surviving from the thirteenth-century Hospital of St John), that led to the foundation in 1877 of the Society for the Protection of Ancient Buildings by William Morris and his friends. Waterhouse was in fact himself one of the founder members of the SPAB, and later of the National Trust, and his buildings demand a more sympathetic examination than they sometimes receive. His career may also be taken as an example of the progressive professionalisation of architecture. We know a great deal about his office because his family presented the whole archive of drawings, ledgers, letters and accounts to the RIBA. Edwin Waterhouse, Alfred's brother, was an accountant and advised him how to establish an efficient book-keeping system. His assistants (a maximum of only thirteen, and in the earlier part of his career between three and five) were draughtsmen rather than designers in their own right and it is clear that all important architectural decisions were Waterhouse's alone. Not surprisingly a number of motifs are re-used from previous buildings and occasionally assistants are asked to trace details from another job. But there is still an astonishing fertility of invention, often with beautifully coloured drawings showing alternatives for façade treatment or pavement decoration. Some sense of the richness of Waterhouse's terracotta detailing can be gained by visiting his 1891 Lloyds Bank (formerly Foster's Bank) at the corner of Sidney Street and Hobson Street. The multi-coloured exterior is impressive enough – the stone pointed end was added in the 1920s. It is hard to imagine the complex sets of drawings that must have been necessary to create the terracotta tiled octagonal interior with its mosaic floor, which was perhaps inspired by San Vitale in Ravenna.

At Pembroke his hall has been altered to a version of the original he demolished, but two of Waterhouse's new buildings nearly abut to form a courtyard – the library of 1875 and the earlier Red Building of 1871–2. This adjoins, with a screen, Wren's chapel (p. 55) and is in complete contrast to it. The Trumpington Street elevation is nearly symmetrical but with significant differences in the detailing of the corbelling to the bay windows which are of unequal height. The decoration is achieved by a selective expression of constructional function: carved gargoyles to shed the water, arched brickwork to relieve the structural loads over openings, projected head moulds to protect the windows below. On the south façade, where there is only one angled window, there is a flank of purely abstract expression: the stripes of red brick and stone are carefully placed with a corbelled gable chimney to form a powerful composition, and a bold contrast to the adjoining Peterhouse Master's Lodge (p. 66).

ALL SAINTS', JESUS LANE

The Church of All Saints (Fig. 21) replaced the medieval church of the same name on Trinity Street almost opposite Trinity College. It was removed to allow for a wider road; already an arch had been made through the tower for pedestrians. But the congregation had also swollen, and this substantial building, which was vested in the care of the Redundant Churches Fund little more than 100 years after its construction, was created to meet a real need for space for worship.

The architect chosen was George Frederick Bodley (1827–1907), together with Pearson, Burgess and Street one of the most gifted of the second generation of Gothic revivalists, and it is an important building both in his œuvre and for the Gothic revival in England generally. Pugin's propaganda, aided by the Ecclesiological movement, had ensured that the style for church architecture was almost invariably not only Gothic but 'English Decorated'. But for the following generation the writings of John Ruskin (1819–1900), particularly *The Stones of Venice* (1851–3) and *The Seven Lamps of Architecture* (1849), were of overwhelming influence. Unlike Pugin, Ruskin was not an architect but a critic, acutely sensitive to atmosphere and a master of rhetoric. His hatred of Renaissance art and his compelling descriptions of Venetian Gothic were accompanied by a series of contradictory hints rather than clear prescriptions as to how nineteenth-century buildings might be designed. But the challenge to architects was irresistible. Burgess, Street, Gilbert Scott, and, as we have seen, Waterhouse, remained more or less faithful to Ruskin, with polychrome masonry and the absorption of multiple foreign sources. Butterfield's Keble College at Oxford (he built nothing in Cambridge) is the clearest example of Ruskinian principles applied to college building. Bodley's earliest work, from 1854, combines French and Venetian influence, but by the 1860s he was becoming more interested in a simpler pre-Ruskinian manner. This further shift in taste, of which Bodley appears to have been an important instigator, was influential on the next generation of church builders, some of whom were Bodley's pupils, and into the twentieth century because Bodley was one of the architectural assessors of the 1903 Liverpool Cathedral competition, won by the young Giles Gilbert Scott, and worked with him in the early stages.

All Saints', Jesus Lane appears just at the watershed: Bodley's 1841 perspective of the building had a decidedly continental air with tall buttresses to the tower intersecting with the base of the spire which has some bands of polychromatic decoration combined with large areas of blank wall. As constructed, however, All Saints' is much more like a plain stone Northamptonshire parish church that has grown organically over a number of years. Rather than taking a single period of English Gothic as his inspiration (as Pugin might have done) or a number of diverse continental sources, Bodley has combined elements from English Gothic of the fourteenth and fifteenth centuries: 'Early English' proportions, Decorated tracery in the openings. Internally, windows in the walls of the nave and south aisle are placed neither opposite each other nor centrally in the bays defined by the roof trusses above, as if the church had been built over a number of years by different hands. Later in the century architects were to do this even more self-consciously: George Devey's houses lay a false trail so that it seems as if a sixteenth-

21 All Saints', Jesus Lane

century manor house has had seventeenth-century additions and eighteenth-century alterations, and this is a game in which Shaw and Lutyens also indulged. There is some evidence that the adoption of English models (of which *The Ecclesiologist*, incidentally, heartily approved) was partly as a result of the powerful influence of Dr Whewell, Master of Trinity, who had already employed Salvin to restore his lodge in Great Court and construct the plain stone neo-Gothic court named after him between Trinity Street and Sidney Street.

The interior of All Saints' is tall and restrained. With no north aisle, and the south aisle nearly as high as the nave, it has a generous volume. Resisting strident 'Victorian' polychromy in the materials, Bodley employed stencilled decoration on the walls and ceilings to his own designs, executed by C. E. Kempe, who is better known for his stained glass of which there are two examples in the north wall of the nave. There is also stained glass by Morris and Co., employing Burne-Jones, Ford Madox Brown and Morris himself, making this one of the most important pre-Raphaelite church interiors in the country. The pulpit (Bodley with Kempe again) is especially fine. Bodley was not a member of the famous pre-Raphaelite brotherhood, the group of artists formed by Millais, Rossetti and Holman Hunt in 1848 and dedicated to the revival of medieval painting, which was much praised by Ruskin. But he was a friend of many of them and worked for much of his career with William Morris on stained glass, tiles, church fittings and wallpaper designs.

Notes on further reading

A classic text on the Gothic revival is Kenneth Clark's *The Gothic Revival*. Useful essays on the nineteenth-century stylistic debate are contained in Pevsner's *Some Architectural Writers of the Nineteenth Century*.

There are monographs on William Wilkins by R. W. Liscombe (1980), and on Thomas Hope (1968) and C. R. Cockerell (1974) by David Watkin. The buildings of Downing College are fully described and illustrated in Cinza Sicca's *Committed to Classicism*. Colin Cunningham and Prudence Waterhouse have published an excellent monograph on Waterhouse and his practice (1992); there is also a useful catalogue edited by Maltby, MacDonald and Cunningham (1983). For Ruskin, there is no substitute for Ruskin's own writing: *The Stones of Venice*, for example.

An excellent description of the work of Bodley and his friends in Cambridge is contained in Duncan Robinson and Stephen Wildman's *Morris and Company in Cambridge*. Stephen Humphrey, Secretary of the Ecclesiological Society, has compiled a history (1983) of the rebuilding of All Saints'.

CHAPTER 7

Late nineteenth- and early twentieth-century eclecticism (1875–1939)

'QUEEN ANNE' STYLE

By the 1870s the high moral tone of Pugin and the Ecclesiologists was losing favour. Something less earnest and rigid was required to meet new needs; the emphasis was on education and on art. In contrast to the aesthetics of Ruskin, whose influential writings had helped to establish Gothic as the prevailing style, Walter Pater (1839-94) declared that aesthetically 'all periods, types, schools of taste, are in themselves equal'. The confident neo-Gothic of Waterhouse and Scott had been identified not only with town halls and law courts but also with commercial buildings like the Prudential Assurance Company. A more delicate style would also accord with the national character. In a letter of 1862 Warrington Taylor, the manager of William Morris' firm, wrote that 'aspiring, grand straining after the extraordinary [was] all very well in France but is wrong here . . . Everything English is essentially small, and of a homely farmhouse kind of poetry.'

Architecturally, therefore, the models are primarily domestic. When William Morris had asked Philip Webb to build him a house in 1859, the result, the famous Red House, was neither Gothic nor classical but looked to vernacular farmhouses for inspiration, as had neo-Gothic architects like Butterfield and Street in their minor domestic buildings such as parsonages. The so-called 'Queen Anne' manner which developed in the 1870s is, in Girouard's description, 'a kind of architectural cocktail . . . with red brick and white-painted sash windows, with curly pedimented gables and delicate brick panels of sunflowers . . . small window panes, steep roofs and curving bay windows', a style publicised by Webb's much more flamboyant contemporary Richard Norman Shaw (1831–1912). He had worked for Street, one of the best Gothic-revivalists and the winner of the Law Courts competition on the Strand, but with his partner Nesfield swiftly moved on to picturesque timber-framed country houses and Dutch 'Queen

Anne', before, towards the end of his life, indulging in grand Edwardian Baroque. Both Champneys, whose work at Newnham is described in more detail below, and J. J. Stevenson began as Goths, but quickly turned eclectic. Of the new houses constructed in the late nineteenth century in west Cambridge, the most skilful and enjoyable are by Stevenson. Balliol Croft, on Madingley Road, now incorporated into Lucy Cavendish College, is a brilliant example with its picturesque handling of parapet and eaves, corbelled chimney stacks, bay windows and verandahs. Stevenson built for Christ's (p. 50) and also converted The Old Granary, on Silver Street. This was later to be the house of Gwen Raverat, the painter and author of one of the most delightful books on Cambridge, *Period Piece*, and is now part of Darwin College. It has a balcony and bay window looking over the Cam. The self-conscious way in which symmetries are established and subtly broken on the river front is characteristically skilful.

THE ARTS AND CRAFTS AND EDWIN LUTYENS

English pre-First World War domestic architecture was much admired abroad. Hermann Muthesius, attached to the German Embassy in London by the Weimar Republic, published a comprehensive survey, *Das Englische Haus*, in 1906. Muthesius returned to the Werkbund, the school of architecture and design based in Weimar, out of which grew the Bauhaus in 1918, when the machine was absorbed within a philosophy of predominantly craft technology, eventually to dominate. But architecture in England after 1918 did not embrace machine technology. The most creative British architects, after the 1851 Great Exhibition when Britain displayed its manufacturing skills to the world in a remarkable pre-fabricated industrial building by Joseph Paxton, had worked within a Morris-inspired craft framework, and were critical of the influence of the machine on architecture. The most admired figure in the generation following Norman Shaw was Edwin Lutyens (1869–1944), whose career has a strangely similar profile to Shaw's. His early work, beginning with the house he designed for the gardener Gertrude Jekyll, was in an Arts and Crafts manner, but with occasional essays in a 'William and Mary' brick classicism. By 1906 he had built in a fully developed Baroque and he went on to create the monumental Imperial Capital of New Delhi from 1913. His building at Benson Court, Magdalene, is well worth visiting. If he had had his way, all of the cottages on Magdalene Street would have been swept away; fortunately only a single wing was built of what was intended to be a large court open to the river. The surviving houses and cottages were later converted and some new buildings inserted; the architect was David Roberts, a fellow of Magdalene, and prolific in Cambridge during the 1960s and 1970s. Lutyens' range has his characteristic combination of sculptural inventiveness (the handling of the chimneys on the river elevation), abstraction (in bringing the windows to the plane of the wall, and all the mouldings in the doors and

Map 6

Ⓐ   Newnham College
Ⓑ   The Law School
Ⓒ   Clare College Memorial Court
     and the University Library
Ⓓ   48, Storey's Way

Other buildings mentioned
①   Balliol Croft
②   The Old Granary
③   Magdalene College Benson Court
④   Zoology Building
⑤   Elmside
⑥   Five Gables

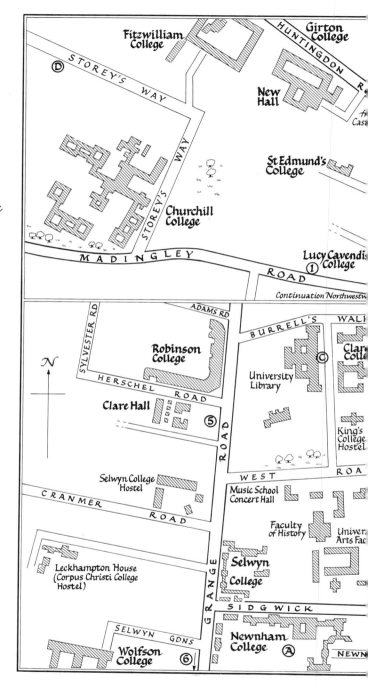

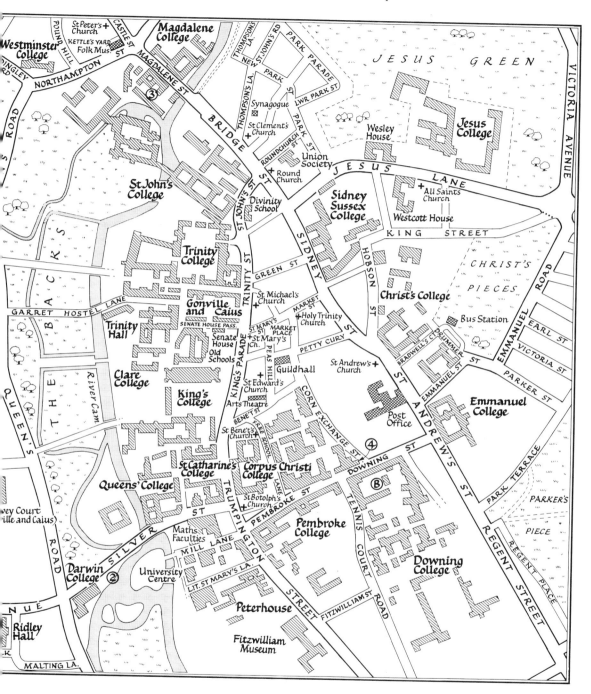

panelling similarly to a flush plane) and a game of classical allusion: each of the newel posts at the bottom of the stairs is different (supposedly so that drunken undergraduates can find their way home in the dark), the most playful being a free interpretation of the pyramidal monument at Halicarnassus from Colonna's *Hypnerotomachia Polyphili*. Lutyens was a brilliant architect who chose to remain within the conventions he inherited rather than to explore and invent new architectural languages: for this he was criticised by some twentieth-century historians, but none have denied his skill within the manner he chose.

Herbert Baker, whose additions to Downing have already been noted, also built at New Delhi, working in a superficially similar style. In Cambridge he designed the pleasant Scott Polar Institute in Lensfield Road, with its splendid engraved inscription on the north façade, and quaintly decorated columns inside – the order of the Penguin.

NEWNHAM COLLEGE

Newnham College is one of the most important and characteristic set of buildings of the 'Queen Anne' revival described above (Fig. 22). Girton, which was the first women's college, had been established in Hitchin before moving to its new buildings near Girton village in 1873. Waterhouse was the architect and it is in his familiar hard red-brick style: only the spiral staircases and the asymmetrical tower of the gatehouse add any relief. Perhaps in deference to the presumed frailty of the young ladies (though Butterfield had done the same at Keble College, Oxford in 1868) the building departs from the Cambridge staircase system to employ internal corridors which are of interminable length. Newnham was altogether more advanced and less authoritarian in its architecture as well as in its educational policy. Champneys built for the college from 1874 until 1910. He based his scheme neither on collegiate staircases nor on institutional corridors, but on the idea of a series of houses. They faced a lane, which was removed in the 1880s when Sidgwick Avenue was laid out. To understand Champneys' concept it is necessary, preferably in summer, to walk into the Gertrude Jekyll garden and to look at the buildings from there: Old Hall (the first to be constructed), the Pfeiffer Building, Sidgwick, Clough (containing the dining room), Kennedy and Peile. Later extensions have partly obscured the 1897 library, and because all of the houses are now connected at ground level along Sidgwick Avenue Girton-like corridors have resulted.

From the garden side, the most striking building is the central Clough Hall, with its pair of enormous oriel windows and single lantern. Here Champneys' playful version of classicism can be observed. High buttresses or plinths support stumpy engaged Ionic columns. The capitals, architraves, friezes and decorative swags are all made of red terracotta. The decorative mouldings run around the bays, where they are translated into white painted timber. Above the cornice are scrolls and each pier ends in a

22 Newnham College, viewed from the gardens

terracotta pinnacle. The character is exuberant, but at the same time precise: everything has been carefully considered and drawn by Champneys, and built under his direction, so that the spontaneity is not the result of the inventive interpretation of the builder but the artifice of the architect.

The Pfeiffer Building is a *tour de force* interpretation of the Cambridge gatehouse. One of the octagonal towers contains bay windows to the major rooms, including that originally inhabited by Eleanor Sidgwick who became Principal in 1892, while the other is a staircase turret. Like Stevenson, Champneys revels in the asymmetry which results.

Champneys and many in his generation saw architecture as an artistic activity rather than a profession or a business. As well as building, he wrote not only several articles in professional journals, but a book about the landscape and architecture around Romney Marsh and a two-volume study, *Memoirs and Correspondence of Coventry Patmore* about the poet who was one of his closest friends. With Bodley, Webb, Shaw, T. G. Jackson and others, he argued that architects ought to be more closely associated with 'the sister arts of painting and sculpture' and that the attempt to make architecture a profession (as the Royal Institute of British Architects, which had been founded in 1837, was campaigning for in 1891) was fundamentally misconceived. In fact, a closed profession has never been achieved; registration of title came only in 1931 but even this was under attack by the 1990s. Certainly, it has been possible for very few privileged architects in the later twentieth century to live up to the artistic ideals espoused by Champneys' generation.

Stylistically, Champneys was more concerned to build in a manner that was appropriate to his clientele than to keep up with the latest fashions. For the Divinity Schools in Cambridge, begun in 1877, he was happy to employ a rich Gothic style, although he had also proposed and stated a preference for a Tudor Renaissance manner. His buildings at Oxford for Mansfield College, New College and Merton College are all Gothic but carefully modulated to their context. The Rylands Library in Manchester (1890–9) is in an elaborate decorated Gothic with a wonderfully intricate interior. Nevertheless his later buildings at Newnham do reflect changing tastes. Kennedy Hall, of 1905, in particular, anticipates the general move towards neo-Georgian of the early decades of the twentieth century. Only the central pair of bays, with their engaged Ionic pilasters, intertwined scrolls and slightly projected windows, echo the earlier more flamboyant work. Champneys did not die until he was 93, in 1935, when his buildings for Newnham, some from as many as sixty years before, must have seemed distinctly old-fashioned. It has proved understandably difficult so far for other architects to add to the college in a manner which respects his combination of dignity and playfulness, robustness and delicacy.

THE LAW SCHOOL COMPLEX

The University's development for the sciences north of Downing Street from the 1860s was haphazard and mostly carried out in a late Victorian eclectic style by renegade former Goths. Along Downing Street itself, running eastwards are stone-faced buildings for Chemistry by J. J. Stevenson and for Zoology by E. S. Prior. The south side was sold to the University by Downing College. This is where Wilkins had planned an entrance avenue leading to his propylaea. It is now occupied by buildings by T. G. Jackson (1835–1924): the Sidgwick Museum of Geology, Law School and Museum of Archaeology and Ethnology. From his *Recollections*, written between 1904 and 1915, but not published until 1950 by his son, we can learn something of the background of a successful nineteenth-century architect and the reasons he gives for the manner he adopts. As an undergraduate at Wadham College, Oxford, Jackson achieved more on the river than he did in the examination room, but he was a talented draughtsman. His father thought he would do better as an architect than as a painter and arranged an interview with his neighbour in Hampstead, George Gilbert Scott, then at the height of his fame. He became Scott's pupil, for a 300 guinea fee, and was trained in severest Gothic ('geometrical decorated' or 'transitional' as he describes it). After two and half years he obtained his first independent commission and in 1862 began a practice of

23 The Law School complex: part of the north façade

church restoration and small country houses. Two years later he was elected to a non-residential fellowship at his old college and this gave him both a measure of financial independence, so that he could travel abroad on sketching tours to study architecture, and also a source of architectural patronage. It was after a trip to Italy in 1864 that he returned 'cured of medievalism'. In 1873 his *Modern Gothic Architecture* urged the union of all the arts, architecture, painting and sculpture. His generation wanted to revive 'not this style or that style . . . but art itself . . . to adopt the language we thought finest'. Jackson's great opportunity came in 1875 with a competition for the Examination Schools in Oxford. One of his fellow competitors was Bodley, who remarked to him, 'I have half a mind after all to do it in Renaissance.' ' "It's quite hopeless", said I "you will only waste your time and spoil your chance". And so I set to work on my design in Gothic and the more I did the less I liked it. The thing wouldn't come at all, and I began to despair. Before my eyes seemed to come the haunting vision of Elizabethan and Jacobean work . . . and finally I gave up all I had done and started afresh in a sort of Renaissance style and everything seemed to go smoothly.' Everyone else made Gothic schemes, but Jackson's aesthetic allowed much more flexibility both of planning and characterisation and he won the day. In the following years Jackson built for many of the Oxford colleges, and in 1897 began his chapel for Giggleswick School, Yorkshire: 'I was determined to show that domes and Gothic architecture are not incompatible.'

The advantages and shortcomings of Jackson's eclecticism are clear to see in his only building in Cambridge, constructed between 1904 and 1911. On the positive side, the massing of the building, which is picturesque but not disordered, is a splendid contribution to the street. His mastery of the complex combination of elements is admirable – the way in which the 'Elizabethan' bays sit on top of the 'sort of Renaissance' cornice at the entrance for example. The brick and stone vaulted porte-cochère leads into a courtyard, where a sculptural external staircase snakes up on the north-east to give access to the Sidgwick Museum under an elaborate Baroque doorcase. Subsidiary internal stairs are expressed in octagonal towers which end in a Jacobean skyline of copper turrets and domes. The balance between the sculptural composition and detailed elaboration, such as the delightful reliefs of mammoths on the north façade, is finely held. The standard of construction is high, the early years of the twentieth century being an excellent period for architectural craftsmanship.

Less convincing are the interiors. The upper floors of the Archaeological Museum form a double-height top-lit space, on the south wall of which stand the remains of Inigo Jones' choir screen for Winchester Cathedral. (Jackson was repairing Winchester and saved this fragment for Cambridge.) It is central to the upper floor but asymmetrically set in relation to the balustraded void. Entering this space on the other axis, the prominent and unusual circular windows are also set askew. In the Sidgwick Museum the junction between the lower north wing and the slightly raised east wing, at an obtuse angle, is negotiated by some broad slate steps and openings either side of a central niche. But the interior columns sit in front of the niche in a thoroughly awkward way. While Jackson's language is scenographically effective, he seems not to have had the necessary skill to manipulate the internal volumes so as to turn a competent (and under-appreciated) building into a memorable work of architecture.

E. S. Prior (1852–1932), whose Zoology Building turns the corner of Downing Street and Corn Exchange Street, is an architect of a different character. He was educated at Harrow School and Gonville and Caius and trained as an architect between 1873 and 1878 in the offices of Richard Norman Shaw, the most successful stylist of his day. One of his earliest buildings designed within his own practice is Henry Martyn Hall (1884–6) in Cambridge for the University Church Missionary Society. Between 1884 and 1891, Prior built extensively for his old school, Harrow, but he is most well known for his extraordinary 'butterfly' house, The Barn at Exmouth (1896). From 1912 to 1932 he held the Slade Professorship of Fine Art at the University, and a Fellowship in Caius, and concentrated on writing and teaching. He founded the University's Department of Architecture and wrote a number of books on Gothic art and architecture.

He tried in his practice to allow materials and construction to have a major effect on form, rather than to indulge in particular stylistic motifs. He built some houses for academics in Cambridge: Elmside, on Grange Road and now part of the graduate college of Clare Hall (p.113), is partly clad in clay tiles. The Zoology Building has a staircase hall with a convincing abstraction to it, and the idea of the circular anatomy room (now a reading room) thrusting its way out diagonally from the rest of the laboratory is a fine one.

CLARE MEMORIAL COURT AND THE UNIVERSITY LIBRARY

Clare College commissioned Sir Giles Gilbert Scott in 1922 to design a new court on their land beyond West Road. It was the first college to build beyond the Backs and for some decades both its position and scale made it awkwardly prominent. Scott obtained the commission for the new University Library some nine years later, while the Memorial Court was still under construction. The two buildings are treated as a single composition and axially aligned. In the mid-1980s an octagonal college library was added by Philip Dowson of Arup Associates in the neck of the college court.

Giles Gilbert Scott (1880–1960), the grandson of the famous nineteenth-century Gothic architect, George Gilbert Scott, achieved early fame in 1903 by winning the competition for the Anglican Cathedral in Liverpool. He was still completing his articles at the time he was appointed to the work jointly with Bodley (see p. 83). By 1910 Scott had completed a total re-design of the cathedral to roughly the form it takes today. (It was completed only in 1980.) Liverpool remains his most original building and set the pattern for most of his subsequent work, in the words of Gavin Stamp 'massive and sublime, almost classical in proportion and in a most personal style of Gothic'. This compromise between the modern and the traditional, the classical tradition and his origins in Gothic, was the result of Scott's self-conscious avoidance of extreme positions. So his most famous building, the now redundant Battersea Power Station of 1930–4, breaks down the enormous bulk of brick masonry by a series of semi-traditional motifs that serve to temper the abstract monumentality of the building as a whole. Something of the same occurs in Memorial Court. The spatial composition is bold and austere but this is modified by somewhat anaemic neo-Georgian detail in reconstructed stone, domesticating the grand triumphal archway, and decorating the entrances to the individual staircases around the court. There seems to be a mis-match between the refinement of the plinths and architraves and the boldness of the overall conception. In this respect the University Library is more successful. It is more abstract and sombre and there is an effective contrast between the vertical strip windows which run in front of six floors of the library stack, and the plainer surfaces of the twelve-storey pyramid-topped tower which sits over the main entrance (Fig. 24). Yet the combination of abstraction, strict symmetry and half-heartedly classical motifs is decidedly uncomfortable. The balance or compromise that Scott is seeking is certainly difficult, and his attempts can be compared to Lutyens' more successful fusion of modernity and tradition at Magdalene, or to the magnificent library for the city of Stockholm (of 1920–8) by E. G. Asplund with its dramatic circular reading room. It has to be acknowledged, however, that Scott's University Library has gained the affection of several generations not merely because of the accessibility of its collection and the convenience of its tea room. There are some splendid interior fittings in the major spaces, while the utilitarian stacks have browsing spaces adjacent to the window slots where it is possible to work with pleasure for days at a time. A more striking and less compromised composition may well have sacrificed the comfort of its users to achieve bolder aesthetic ends, and perhaps that is why the latest in the series of extensions to the library is carried out to match the pattern of the original building exactly. As at Battersea Power Station, Scott seems to have succeeded in designing an enormous and potentially alienating building in a way which inspires sympathy and affection. Gradually with the continuing growth of new college and faculty buildings around, Scott's library with its dominant central tower, and its pendant symmetrical Memorial Court, has begun to act as a powerful anchor to the whole of west Cambridge.

Members of the 30s Society were among those who objected to the insertion of Philip Dowson's library for Clare College in front of the University Library Tower, closing off Memorial Court. In some ways the new building has improved the approach to the University Library: the previously banal processional route, dominated by the looming tower, has been diverted into a pair of paths around the new building and under small baldacchinos. This is not to say that the new building is unproblematic. As an object, it is too large to read as a pavilion in the space, but too strong a centroidal form to be perceived primarily as a wall to the court. This is an ambiguity that is strengthened by the removal of the entrance from the east (the approach from the rest of the college). One is greeted by a severe and unadorned brick wall. The college was unable to agree to the architect's proposal for a pool in this position. Instead, the entrance is on the west where it faces the steps of the University Library. Here the façade, which is elsewhere of simple silver-grey brick with stone cornices to match Scott's, is columned with ashlar stonework above, in a close quotation (but seven bays, not five) of Brunelleschi's 1429 Pazzi Chapel in Florence.

Internally, the main library occupies a generous half-octagon facing east and is preceded by a small hallway of two-storey volume under an oculus. There is a clear reference to the sequence of spaces in the college's eighteenth-century chapel. The music practice rooms make up the wings of the building and are elaborately separated structurally to ensure acoustic privacy. The somewhat perverse enjoyment in over-coming technical problems like these, as well as the stylistic self-consciousness and formal ambiguities, make this a 'Mannerist' building in the sense that the term was

24 The University Library

applied to the work of those architects of the Italian Renaissance who succeeded the heroic generation of the High Renaissance (p. 40). Sir Philip Dowson of Arup Associates (himself a graduate of Clare) designed a significant building in Cambridge early in his career, Leckhampton House for Corpus Christi. Here the language is one of 'heroic' structural expression, an exposition of frame and skin, with services and staircases behind solid brick walls. Twenty years later, at Clare, many of the enriching contradictions that particularise older environments, and that orthodox Modernism endeavoured to suppress, have been embraced. What has been lost is the appealing clarity of expression which seems, in retrospect, to have been a reflection of a less complicated and more optimistic world.

48 STOREY'S WAY

One of the English architects working at the turn of the century that Hermann Muthesius most admired was Mackie Hugh Baillie Scott (1865–1945). Though he is now less well known than Voysey, Lutyens or Charles Rennie Mackintosh, in the early years of the twentieth century, because of the considerable publicity given to his work in *The Studio* he was at least as famous. He began practice in the Isle of Man in 1889, but by 1901 had moved to Bedford, only some 30 miles west of Cambridge. His architectural work is almost exclusively domestic, and for J. P. White of Bedford he also designed furniture. His first Cambridge house, published in his influential *Houses and Gardens* of 1906, is Five Gables at 4 Grange Road. It introduces the theme that was to preoccupy him all his career and about which he writes with some eloquence in *Houses and Gardens* – the idea of 'homeliness'. This is achieved by arranging the spaces to interlock both with each other, by the use of double doors or sometimes internal windows, and with the outdoors so that house and garden are conceived as a single entity. Principal rooms are built around the twin foci of a fireplace, which is often contained within an inglenook, like a room within a room, and a bay window addressing the garden. There is a careful control of orientation, so that bedrooms preferably face east, service rooms like bathrooms and larders are on the north and living spaces face south.

Later in his career, when he had moved to London and entered into partnership with Beresford, Baillie Scott built twelve more houses in and around Cambridge, four of them in Storey's Way. Of these number 48, of 1912–13, is the finest, and a characteristic example of his work (Fig. 25). On the north side, facing the road, the steep pitched roof sweeps down to single-storey wings containing larders and outhouses. On the south a nearly symmetrical two-storey elevation faces the garden. The simple arrangement, with a corridor on part of the ground and most of the first floor running along the back of the plan, allows a series of rooms to face south over the garden and is enriched by numerous subtle touches. Behind the main living space, to the east, lies a study whose bays and recesses are precisely fashioned to make comfortable places to read and write. The twin bays to the garden, from dining room and living room, are divided by a doorway connecting the central pathway which runs from the front gate via the porch and is aligned with the formally planned garden on the south. But this line is not absolutely straight, in the same way as the south façade is not absolutely symmetrical and the plastered ceilings and carved oak balustrades retain a hand-crafted irregularity. For Baillie Scott, and architects of his generation, machine-like regularity either in planning or in the finish of materials was anathema. At the same time, he manages to avoid the coyness and sentimentality into which self-conscious Arts and Crafts revivalism often degenerates: partly this is because of the sparseness of the decoration – simple elaboration of the ceiling plaster in one or two rooms and some embossed leadwork. It is a mistake to see the plainness of the English Free School, as these architects came to be known, either as heralding the abstraction of Modernism or as merely indulging in a romantic vernacular revivalism. For the future holds many possibilities. In the latter half

25 The living room and dining room of 48 Storey's Way

of the twentieth century cheap fuel made it economical to carry factory-produced building materials all over the country or import them from abroad, so that an architecture which depends for its effect on indigenous materials and skilled craftsmanship looks distinctly old-fashioned. Yet a growing concern in recent decades for energy conservation makes the English Free School philosophy seem much more plausible. Clay tiles (burnt at lower temperatures than concrete), oak joinery (from indigenous renewable resources) and lime plasters (able to 'breathe' and withstand movement much more easily than cement-based renders) are no less suitable for not being 'modern' and, like real ale, may be enjoyed for their authentic flavour in contrast to the artificial taste of much twentieth-century building.

Notes on further reading

Mark Girouard's *Sweetness and Light*, in which Warrington Taylor's letter is quoted, discusses the 'Queen Anne' Movement from 1860 to 1900, with a chapter on Newnham College and the houses of J. J. Stevenson. In 1989 Newnham College published a booklet by David Watkin entitled *The Architecture of Basil Champneys*. One of the best accounts of the debate about professionalism, and the changed status of architects during the nineteenth and twentieth centuries, is to be found in Andrew Saint's *The Image of the Architect*, particularly chapters 3, 5 and 7.

The Dilemma of Style by J. Mordaunt Crook discusses the 'progressive eclecticism' of the late nineteenth century; the thoroughly readable *Recollections of Thomas Graham Jackson* was published by Oxford University Press in 1950.

A monograph on M. H. Baillie Scott by J. D. Kornwolf was published in 1972, but his own two volumes entitled *Houses and Gardens* of 1908 and 1936 are more rewarding. *The Architect's Journal* of 22 July 1992 records the repair of 48 Storey's Way with an article by Diane Haigh.

For Gilbert Scott see the essay 'Sir Giles Gilbert Scott' by Gavin Stamp in *Sir Gilbert Scott and the Scott Dynasty* edited by Roger Dixon (1980).

CHAPTER 8

Post-war buildings
(1939–1970)

THE LANGUAGE OF MODERNISM

It is a truism that the pace of change accelerates. While building technology changed very little between, say, 1400 and 1600, in the last fifty years profound social and economic changes in our society have naturally been reflected in its technology and its architectural expression. One aspect of the social revolution has been the motor vehicle, and that has changed the setting of buildings; another has been the arrival of cheap machine-made products referred to at the end of the previous chapter. Allied to this a more proper remuneration of the workforce has made on-site craftsmanship relatively more expensive. Particularly in the decades immediately after the Second World War, when building was limited by government licence, it was nearly impossible to build in a traditional manner even if architects had been inclined to do so. Yet, partly because of the continuing need to repair ancient buildings, some traditional skills survived, so that given a generous enough budget, architects in the second half of the twentieth century could call upon these as well as on new technologies.

Many of the changes that were to occur, socially and stylistically, were anticipated by polemical architects on the continent before the First World War and given a concrete image in the 1920s. It was possible to make buildings like machines, and Le Corbusier, the most vocal and talented architect of the generation proclaimed this, though not without a certain ambivalence, for he was fully aware of the classic tradition that he saw it as essential to subvert, if architecture was to be preserved as an art and not merely to be replaced by 'building' in an age of mechanisation. If the classical language of architecture took two hundred years to reach England from Italy, Modernism in reaching this country only in the 1930s, mostly as a result of *émigré* architects, was, in the accelerated timescale of the twentieth century, comparably delayed. The formal procedures of Modernism are not as clearly described as those of the classical language

Map 7

Ⓐ Gonville and Caius College
     Harvey Court
Ⓑ History Faculty
Ⓒ St John's College Cripps Building
Ⓓ Clare Hall

Other buildings mentioned
① Mond Laboratory
② Peterhouse Fen Court
③ Churchill College
④ Robinson College
⑤ Queens' College Cripps Court

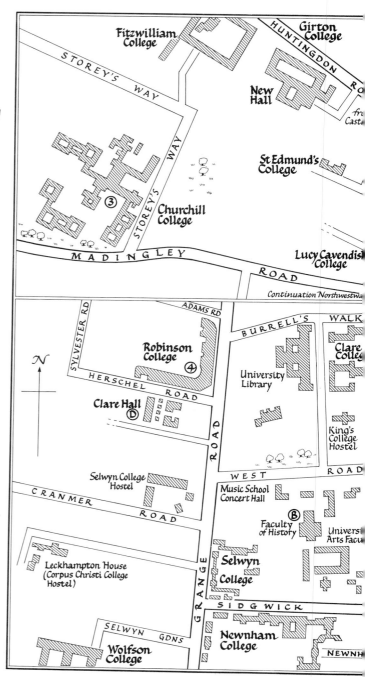

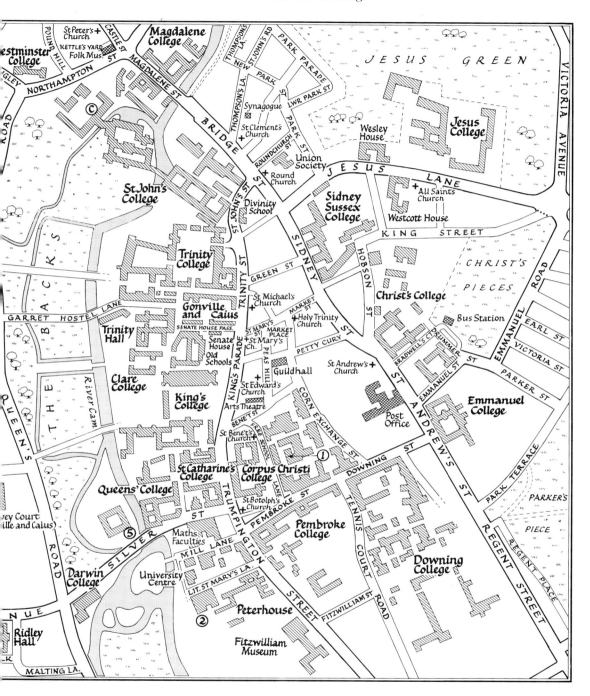

in the pattern-books produced by Serlio and others but there are principles that have their origin in questions of technique, the provision of appropriate forms for new uses and the symbolisation of a vision of a more open and democratic society. The use of a steel or concrete frame, for example, permits windows to be made of continuous strips of glass rather than being holes in a solid masonry wall. Instead of getting progressively more massive as they reach the ground, twentieth-century buildings can be poised over a free-flowing space. A new tri-partite arrangement emerges: in contrast to the rusticated base, vertically proportioned 'piano nobile' and attic storey of the classical building we find an open ground floor with slender columns, or 'piloti', horizontally ordered upper levels and a flat rooftop which can be planted as a garden. This formula is more successful in isolated buildings (such as Le Corbusier's famous Villa Savoye) than in constrained urban sites. Much of the effort of architects in the last quarter of the twentieth century was directed towards finding ways in which the canon of Modernism, which has persuasive virtues in terms of building economy and flexibility, could be accommodated to the context of the pre-twentieth-century city.

MODERNISM IN CAMBRIDGE

The Werkbund which the anglophile Muthesius (see p. 87) had helped to establish in Germany was transformed, as I mentioned, into the famous Bauhaus. In 1935 its former Director, Walter Gropius, came to England as an exile and entered into partnership with Maxwell Fry. Together they built a pair of houses in Kensington, and the Village College at Impington, a few miles north of Cambridge, and planned in 1936–7 an extension to Christ's College that the Fellows rejected. Despite his importance as a teacher (he went on to be the head of the Graduate School of Design in Harvard) Gropius was not nearly as brilliant an architect as Le Corbusier, as the buildings he later designed, within a partnership entitled The Architects' Collaborative, in America and elsewhere testify. Nevertheless it is a pity that Christ's lost this opportunity: Albert Richardson's anaemic Chancellor's Building and Memorial Building, completed between 1948 and 1953, are no substitute. Apart from some interesting houses in west Cambridge and particularly Conduit Head Road, two buildings by H. C. Hughes are the best illustration of the modern movement up until the Second World War – the diminutive Mond Laboratory of 1935 and Fen Court, Peterhouse (with his partner Peter Bicknell) of 1939–40. At Peterhouse the 'piloti' are of brick, the long strip windows are interrupted by wide piers and the roofs have never received the planting they deserve, but the building has an authentic ship-like quality, moored at the edge of the college adjacent to the Fen, and captures something of the heroic and optimistic freshness of the best of the modern movement.

During the 1960s, and partly stimulated by the 1963 Robbins Report on the expansion of higher education, Cambridge experienced one of its periodic building booms. Seven new colleges were founded, three of them for the growing graduate and research population, between 1954 and 1974. A comparison between Churchill College (founded in 1958) and Robinson College of 1974, named after its founder David Robinson, indicates the way in which post-war architecture developed. Reviewing the results of the competition in 1959, Colin Rowe perceptively described the problem for the post-war architect, trained in a 'democratic' Modernist mode, of expressing 'a society animated by a common mystique, dedicated primarily to scientific pursuits, implicated with the name of a great and volatile conservative statesman . . . to stand in certain functional and symbolic relationships with the University, the country and the world'. Stirling and Gowan were praised for their intransigence and aloofness, Howell for his unique and intricate solution. The winning scheme he regarded as 'neat, tidy, bland, well-intentioned and cautious'. With the exception of Alison and Peter Smithson nearly all the architects proposed courtyards but this, for Rowe, constituted a problem: how can the architect deal with 'the intrusion in the enclosing wall surface of a variety of large elements, chapels, dining halls, libraries which are difficult to bring into any relationship with the student sets which provide the basic unit of scale'?

Superficially, as built by Richard Sheppard Robson and Partners, Churchill resembles the traditional college pattern, since the rooms are grouped around court-yards. But in fact the courts, whose rooms are mostly lifted on brick piloti above an open ground floor, are like dormitory suburbs, exclusively residential satellites to the main complex of dining room and offices. There is a separate block containing a library and theatre. Students 'commute' between their rooms, their work and recreation in a manner which recalls, in miniature, the rationalised separation of function in the twentieth-century city proposed by CIAM (the Congrès Internationaux des Architectes Modernes). In its detailed treatment, too, Churchill goes out of its way to display 'truth' to its construction and materials. Primary beams are in-situ reinforced concrete and have weathered to a creamish colour while secondary structure is pre-cast, and is whiter or greenish where it has been stained by the run-off from copper roofs. Strips of window occur at high level to emphasise which walls are load-bearing and which are non-structural. The elevations seem to be the result of this display and nothing more. As a number of critics have pointed out, 'brutalist' buildings of the 1960s represent some of the clearest examples of the built application of Pugin's moral arguments of the 1830s.

In contrast Robinson College, by Metzstein and MacMillan of the Glasgow practice Gillespie Kidd and Coia, attempts to reassert the arrangement and even the imagery of the traditional college. The highly compressed court, at first floor level, is approached up a ramp and under a gateway which looks as if it might contain a portcullis. Off this space come rooms, offices, the chapel, library, dining hall and a theatre. The building forms a dense perimeter around the large garden, though it is difficult to perceive this because the architects have denied the traditional axial progression from court to garden. Brickwork and tiling are draped over the concrete frame structure without regard to the 'truthfulness' or otherwise of their technical expression. Motifs from a thick-walled masonry architecture are used for their expressive possibilities, to emphasise the entrance to the chapel, for example and to give a sculptural depth to the window reveals of the library. By the mid-1970s architects had lost faith in the certainties of twentieth-century technology and were searching for ways to endow their forms with meanings which did more than just refer to the means of their own construction. In the case of Robinson, the result may be socially successful but seems formally effortful in comparison to the adjacent Clare Hall, discussed in more detail below, which is a relaxed composition, obviously 'modern' and undogmatic in its expression.

GONVILLE AND CAIUS COLLEGE HARVEY COURT

Some buildings are more important for the ideas that they represent than for the particular solution that the architect provides to the client's requirements. It could be said that the occupants become guinea pigs for a social experiment, yet without such experiments, one might argue, architectural possibilities can never be fully explored since architects, unlike product designers, cannot have the benefit of a full-scale prototype before putting their designs into production. Harvey Court is one such prototypical building (Fig. 26). Its architect, Leslie Martin, was Professor of Architecture at the University at the time of its design; Colin St. John Wilson, who was working in association with him then, was subsequently the architect of the British Library in London and succeeded him as Professor some years later; Patrick Hodgkinson, who worked with them both and was the co-architect with Martin of this project, went on to hold a personal chair in architecture at the University of Bath.

Martin was preoccupied with ideas of urban planning. As London County Council Deputy Architect he had been responsible for much of the best post-war housing and school building in London, including the highly praised Roehampton West where Corbusian slab blocks on piloti are placed in echelon on a parkland landscape. But Martin was dissatisfied with the mixed-development orthodoxy which had emerged, and especially the assumption encouraged by government that residential tower blocks were the most economical and efficient solution to the housing problem. He founded the Centre for Land Use and Built Form Studies in Cambridge (later re-named the Martin Centre) to investigate the effect on densities of different patterns of urban development. Leaning on the geometrical theories of the French mathematician, Fresnal, he argued that development around the perimeter of sites was more efficient than high-rise towers, was more appropriate for family life, because people could live

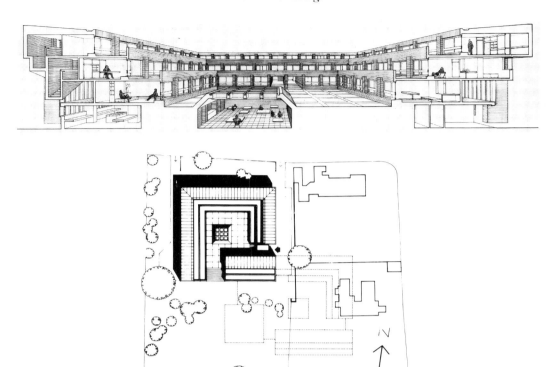

26 Gonville and Caius College Harvey Court: section perspective and site plan showing
intended expansion

closer to the ground, and would create a better environment with sheltered traffic-free
courtyard spaces. It can be no accident that such ideas emerged in Cambridge, a city
of courts. Martin's ideas are applicable at the largest scale, in the planning of new
settlements along transportation routes rather than as separate satellites to existing towns
for example, but they also find echoes in his plans for buildings.

In 1957 King's College had commissioned a study for their site in Market Hill;
Martin designed a scheme for about fifty undergraduates stepped back around a raised
courtyard so that the upper-floor rooms used the roof of the rooms below as a terrace.
The court itself was conceived as being appropriate for outdoor theatre and the
cross-wall construction of the rooms was carried down to form shops which faced the
streets around. Unfortunately King's chose not to proceed with the scheme,
redeveloping the land between themselves and St Catharine's instead, with dismal
results. Harvey Court of 1960–2 for Gonville and Caius College was Martin's next
opportunity to investigate his idea.

The suburban West Road site is a much less suitable location for the urban model – the undercroft of the stepped section becomes car parking instead of shops; most of the rooms are denied a view of the gardens in favour of a prospect across the paved court-yard. The graduated sequence of entry seems perverse in this location: from the severe north elevation, down the flank and up on to the paved court, through to the rear of the block which has a continuous long gallery, up the externally expressed staircases and finally into a room overlooking the court. The rigorous, not to say ruthless, application of the notion of perimeter planning is, however, accompanied by an unusual sculptural sensitivity. In 1935 the critic Adrian Stokes had observed the difference between sculptures that were carved and those that were modelled, whichever the technique actually employed: in this sense Donatello is a modeller even if his technique is some-times one of carving into the stone. Harvey Court appears to have been carved from a solid block of masonry (even though we know it has been built up out of small components) and the position and depth of every cut has been most carefully considered. It is unfortunate that during a refurbishment in the late 1980s the brick paving on the terrace was replaced by pre-cast concrete slabs, because the impression inside the court was equally powerful. The cantilevered stairs on the outside of the court may derive from the staircases the Finnish architect, Alvar Aalto, designed for his student residence Baker House in 1948, for MIT, in Boston, Massachusetts, and Aalto had also used a raised courtyard in his miniature civic centre at Säynätsalo in Finland. But Aalto's geometries are always softened and elided, and his courtyard at Säynätsalo flows out informally into the landscape, where Harvey Court has a broad and severe flight of steps. Since Martin never saw his buildings as isolated objects, but as illustrations of a more general idea, they tend to establish a grid-like pattern across the site in which further buildings can be inserted. To the west is the Music Faculty also by Martin, which was built in a number of phases, in the same facing brick and using a similar structural rhythm. Harvey Court itself was designed to be extended, and indeed it may come into its own, as a kind of acropolis, when Caius develops the adjacent gardens for further residential accommodation as intended. Its strength, however, remains as a model for urban ideas; it was published internationally as soon as it was completed and sprouted imitations in Europe and America.

THE HISTORY FACULTY

James Stirling's History Faculty (Fig. 27) in West Road is the most controversial building to have been erected in Cambridge since the war. Much admired by architects (it won an RIBA award in 1968), it was criticised by its occupants and members of the University from the day it was finished.

The University Grants Committee, following lobbying by the Faculty over a

27 Main reading room of the History Faculty

considerable number of years, decided in 1962 to give money for a new library provided that it could be spent within the next two financial years. Stirling was one of three architects considered in a competition held that winter (the start on site had to be before 31 March 1964), the others being David Roberts and the Architects' Co-partnership. With his partner James Gowan, Stirling was engaged on a new Engineering building for the University of Leicester, arguably the masterpiece of the early part of his career, and the astonishing inventiveness of the forms employed in that building no doubt commended his candidature to the committee even though the University Grants Commission was unhappy at his appointment because of technical problems at Leicester. He had placed the teaching spaces in red brick towers, off which were hung two sculpturally expressive lecture theatres, and contrasted with these was a large workshop block with factory north lights made of 'patent glazing', a proprietary system of aluminium bars holding glass. The patent glazing snakes up the tower as well as covering the workshop areas. At the History Faculty building a similar strategy is employed. An L-shape of offices and seminar rooms, with the same red brick as Leicester on the gable ends, encloses a quadrant-shaped two-storey library, like a quarter of a Benthamite panopticon. Patent glazing is draped over the whole, in two skins over the library proper, the void between the two containing the supporting trusses. No account is taken of the neighbouring buildings on the Sidgwick site, by Casson Condor and Partners; the building draws its inspiration from nineteenth-century industrial buildings as well as from the sculptural expressionism of the early twentieth century.

What is shocking, in a library, is the denial of the sense of propriety that Cockerell, by the manipulation of an inherited classical language, achieved in the former University Library in Senate House Passage (pp. 78–80), and which Scott struggled to represent at his University Library (pp. 95–7). Can it be appropriate to dress a library in the same clothes as an Engineering Faculty? If there is no language to inherit, has Stirling succeeded in suggesting a new paradigm (to use the term mentioned in the introduction, p. 4)? Then there have been technical shortcomings: an absence of soundproofing between seminar rooms, movements between differing parts of the structure, the performance of the red tiles (now replaced by bricks, much to the detriment of the proportions of the towers), heat losses through the glazing in winter and unacceptable heat gains in summer. Less than twenty years after its construction, the University even considered demolishing the building rather than face the cost of immediate and continuing repairs.

Stirling, who died, still in his prime, in 1992, was certainly one of those few architects who forge new languages rather than accept an inherited manner. The History Faculty building was published internationally when it was completed and has been a place of pilgrimage for architects ever since. By employing a technology that had previously been thought suitable only for industrial sheds or greenhouses to clad a library, in forms of seductive sculptural power, he opened the way for imitators, especially in Germany and Japan, to make similar experiments; this in turn led to a demand for glazing systems that could perform to more stringent criteria and these increasingly sophisticated technologies swiftly became cheaper, so that not only the glass-atriumed shopping centre and office building of the 1980s but also the adjacent Law Faculty building by Norman Foster could use an economical technology, that was unavailable to Stirling in 1968, precisely because he had imagined its possibility. If Stirling was irresponsible to his immediate client (given the constraints of budget and timetable to which he was subject), he could in this sense be said to have fulfilled a larger responsibility to architecture as a whole. Even if his building had remained an isolated icon of a failed experiment it would have an historical importance as part of the œuvre, though by no means the masterpiece, of one of the most inventive British architects of the twentieth century.

After the 1960s, Stirling's best work was abroad. At the Staatsgalerie extension in Stuttgart, he produced the most convincing argument in the post-war era for an expanded architectural vocabulary, embracing historical references to many periods with consummate facility. His procedures are indebted to Modernism: the Corbusian *promenade architecturale* – the idea of a route through a building as a determinant of its form – the free shapes of Alvar Aalto, and the technological expressionism of 'high tech' architecture. But Modernism is quoted with irony, and Stirling also plays with neo-classical motifs and the compositional methods of the past.

The approach to the History Faculty is from the north, off West Road. This was not Stirling's original intention, but the site was altered after the competition and with a characteristic pragmatism he rotated his winning submission with minimal alteration to fit the new location. Since the building is seen as a free-standing object, as a machine, almost, in the axonometric drawings by the architect, it can sustain such a violent re-disposition. A single mushroom-headed column stands at the focus of the library space and from the desk below it the radiating stacks can be surveyed: this ease of supervision was one of the factors that won Stirling the competition. The glazed roof gives a remarkably even quality of light to the central open reading area with its cork tiles and bentwood Thonet chairs. Perimeter reading is provided beyond the stacks for those for whom the central space is too open and public. The arrangement of the library, with these two types of reading space and access past a central control desk, is possibly derived from the thinking of Leslie Martin (who had recommended Stirling as one of the competitors) and who designed a number of university libraries, including a cluster of three on this pattern at Manor Road, Oxford. Corridors to the faculty rooms above pass from outside to become interior glazed galleries overlooking the main library space and by this means the whole faculty is centred, spatially and symbolically, on its principal volume and most visible scholarly activity. At the apex of the roof hang enormous fans to evacuate the hot air between the two skins of glass – formally dramatic, though functionally, as it turns out, quite inadequate.

ST JOHN'S COLLEGE CRIPPS BUILDING

This substantial extension to St John's (Fig. 28) bears the name of its benefactor, Humphrey Cripps. He also funded major extensions at Queens' College (the first phase of which was by Powell and Moya, the architects of the St John's building, the second and less successful phase being by other architects), and a disappointing flint-faced block for Selwyn. St John's is the most successful of his generous benefactions, and Powell and

Moya's best building in Cambridge. It is particularly English in its sensitivity to landscape and its successfully casual and picturesque use of the Modernist vocabulary.

In 1961 Leslie Martin had been invited by the college to study a number of sites, recommend one which would accommodate up to 200 undergraduates and suggest names of potential architects. He visited Alvar Aalto in Finland that year and asked him if he would be interested, but Aalto declined, because he was already over-committed and because he felt he would be unable to control the detailed design at a distance. The choice eventually was between Denys Lasdun, the architect for the new Fitzwilliam College, and Powell and Moya, who had built a successful addition to Brasenose College, Oxford in 1962. Submissions to a well-considered brief and for an agreed fee were invited from both practices. Lasdun proposed four pyramidal blocks linked by covered ways with student rooms around the perimeter enclosing larger spaces such as squash courts. He was later to employ a similar strategy for the residential blocks at the University of East Anglia, and in a modified form for Christ's College.

Powell and Moya's scheme was quite different. Sets of undergraduate rooms off central staircases are lifted above a continuous ground-floor walkway and laid end to end to form a continuous block which snakes its way from the River Cam behind Rickman's New Court, across the Bin Brook and around the twelfth-century School of Pythagoras (p. 11). The arrangement is thus simultaneously 'traditional', in that recognisable courtyards are formed, and 'modern' in that the arrangement obeys the formal principles outlined briefly above. The roof top, which is accessible and can be used for parties, has sculptural penthouse Fellows' rooms as well as lead-cased water tanks creating a romantic skyline. The proportions of the bay windows with their carefully shaped spandrels, sliding bronze windows and fixed lead panels, are particularly successful. The rooms themselves are generous and well-lit and the detailing of doors, gates and external works is sensitive and thoughtful.

For these reasons, on its completion this building was probably the most popular modern building in Cambridge. But despite a generous initial budget there have been technical problems. Flat-roof technology only became reliable in England in the 1980s, when, ironically, college building committees had begun to insist on pitched roofs. Particularly troublesome was the cobbled roof of the single storey common room, and this was demolished in 1987 to be replaced by the Fisher Building (not by Powell and Moya), an overscaled and unsympathetic intrusion in the court despite its attempts at matching the materials of the Cripps Building. The underfloor heating, which used embedded electric coils as specifically requested by the college, has also proved troublesome. Buildings in the past often had generous spaces and high ceiling heights and as new services are required they can be equipped with reasonable ease. In the later twentieth century architects have had to justify every cubic metre of the space they propose and have struggled to integrate servicing with the structure and fabric, often

28 St John's College Cripps Building

without taking full account of their differing life spans. If services are to be given their proper place it has a major effect on the planning of buildings for even relatively under-serviced uses such as accommodation: one of the architects to understand this was the American, Louis Kahn. A danger is that buildings may emerge which display their servicing as the major component of their architecture (the Lloyds Building in London or Centre Pompidou in Paris, both by Richard Rogers, are witness to that), with a resultant semantic confusion. It was one of the achievements of the architects of the Cripps Building that they found a form of expression for their building that is both picturesque and recognisably of its period, appropriately domestic and yet sufficiently dignified to stand up to its challenging historic context.

CLARE HALL

Ralph Erskine, the English-born Swedish architect of Clare Hall, was born in 1914 and educated at the Friends School, Saffron Walden, some 15 miles south of Cambridge. He emigrated to Sweden in 1939, and from 1956 was an articulate member of Team X, a group of young architects who attempted to humanise dogmatic Modernism. In antithesis to the reductive separation of functions proposed by CIAM, of which Churchill College, briefly described above, can be seen as an example, members of Team X laid emphasis on ideas of identity and association, qualities which older environments, particularly the streets and squares of towns and villages, appear to possess in contrast to the aridity of many twentieth-century environments. At the same time, unlike the Postmodernists of later decades, they did not see the problem as primarily one of style or symbolism: there is a confidence that modern materials and inventive forms, sensitively handled, can provide as good an architecture as that of the past without resorting to stylistic imitation. Most of Erskine's work has been in Sweden, but he built the well-known Byker Wall at Newcastle, housing at Newmarket and Milton Keynes, and more recently the Ark office building at Hammersmith, West London.

Clare Hall is founded on a social model of an academic village. There are two pedestrian streets, or walks, running north–south from Herschel Road to Rifle Range Road. The eastern (Scholars' Walk) passes the bar and common room before encountering a doorway which leads to the main social areas and a courtyard of study spaces and seminar rooms. The western or Family Walk (Fig. 29) is bounded by a block of flats which is five storeys high on the north and two storeys on the south. The rooms have west-facing balconies. Between the Family Walk and the Scholars' Walk, which are connected by a narrow passage, lie the Fellows' houses, single storey except for the President's Lodge whose first floor cantilevers over, in a gesture that is dramatic but also, characteristically, understated, to form gateways to the two walks. The village-like college apparently sits on a shallow south-facing slope, formed by the half-sunken car park, and is a compact rectangular closely woven carpet of buildings. At its inauguration there were only six Fellows and thirty-two graduates. As numbers have grown, more graduate students have been housed off the site. A new fifteen-room block, the Michael Stoker Building, has been added to the west and there are plans for further studies in the garden between Clare Hall and Elmside, the house by Edward Prior on Grange Road, and more accommodation in the garden opposite the Stoker Building. Unlike many buildings from the 1960s Clare Hall has not suffered disfiguring alterations.

Throughout the college the intricate plan, which could become confusing, is bound together by using the roof rather than the floor as a datum. From the dining room through the two-level combination room to the seminar and study court, a continuous gently sloping aluminium pitched roof runs from north to south. Its underside is timber boarded in the major spaces, which open on to an east-facing courtyard. Erskine's aesthetic allows considerable freedom in the placing of windows in walls, picturesquely arranged but nearly always making good sense from the interior, and the pragmatic use of structure: cross walls for sound insulation, circular concrete columns in the car park and delicate laminated timber columns for the roof over the common rooms. The

29 Clare Hall, the Family Walk

rainwater over the large roof area is collected in giant metal-lined laminated timber chutes, which discharge in a few carefully chosen places: one makes a pool, during heavy rain, in the Family Walk, creating a paddling place for children. Clare Hall's deliberately unmonumental quality is in refreshing contrast to the pompous rigidity of much twentieth-century building for colleges.

Notes on further reading

For a perceptive essay on the profound changes in British society since the war see Peter Laslett's *The World We Have Lost*; a recent journalistic overview is Brian Appleyard's *The Pleasures of Peace*.

Of the many general surveys of twentieth-century architecture the most approachable is William Curtis' *Modern Architecture since 1900*.

Essential for post-war Cambridge is *Cambridge New Architecture*, which ran to three editions between 1964 and 1970. Its author, Nicholas Taylor, was an undergraduate at Trinity Hall, and his descriptions are accurate and criticisms often perceptive, whilst also illustrating the concerns of the period. He laments the absence of industrialised methods in all but a very few buildings, and architects are frequently called to task for their untruthfulness: 'there is insufficient clarity between load-bearing and non load-bearing brickwork in the service tower', he complains about one building by David Roberts on Castle Hill. The influence of Pugin's ethical critique of architecture in the twentieth century is charted in David Watkin's *Morality and Architecture*. For a passionate and personal view of post-war architecture in Cambridge, constructed or under consideration, see Hugh Plommer's *The Line of Duty*. Rowe's essay on the Churchill Competition 'The Blenheim of the Welfare State' appeared in *The Cambridge Review* of 31 October 1959. Recent non-university buildings of interest for which there is no space in this volume are illustrated in McKean's *Architectural Guide to Cambridge and East Anglia since 1920*.

Adrian Stokes refers to the differences between 'carving' and 'modelling' in a chapter entitled 'Stone and Clay' in *The Stones of Rimini*; a useful collection of Stokes' essays is in Richard Wollheim's *The Image in Form*. For Martin's theories of land use and perimeter planning see *Urban Space and Structures* of 1972. Monographs have been published on James Stirling (compiled by Arnell and Bickford, 1984) and Ralph Erskine (by Peter Collymore, 1982), and by Martin himself (1983). A. C. Crook, the Domestic Bursar at St John's during the period, has printed a full account of the construction of the Cripps Building in his 1978 *Penrose to Cripps*.

CHAPTER 9

Buildings since 1970

Two buildings have been chosen to illustrate the continuing issues of architectural style and patronage in Cambridge. One is to meet a 'traditional' brief, that of a college chapel; the other is for a research institute attached to the University Chemistry Department. Both represent a concern for context, and a highly self-conscious manipulation of architectural language. They are neither more nor less typical of the architecture of the city as a whole than any of the other examples in the book. During the 1980s, as in any period of considerable building activity, much of what was constructed was mediocre. But good buildings must always be the result of enlightened patronage and, in England in the last quarter of the twentieth century, faith in the skills of architects seemed to have diminished, probably in reaction to the heady days in the 1960s when some politicians as well as architects believed that bold architecture would in itself solve social problems and that the public could be educated into a fondness for unprecedented forms. The swing of the pendulum has sometimes been extreme; Downing, for example, erected four buildings by Quinlan Terry in versions of a revivalist classical style around its restrained nineteenth-century neo-classical campus (albeit with substantial pre-war additions by Baker) rather than trust an architect to interpret its needs in a manner that, while sympathetic to its context, would be more representative of its time. That does not mean to say, of course, that excellent buildings, even masterpieces, cannot be produced by architects working in a revisited style: the history of architecture and indeed this book is full of such examples, but they have to be able to manipulate the language with conviction and skill whether they are fully conversant with its grammar, as was Wren or Lutyens for instance, or struggling to learn its syntax, as the architect of the Christ's Fellows' Building seems to have been. The most distressing example of a bad building in period dress is the grotesque Holiday Inn; it stands in Downing Street nearly opposite Jackson's Law School and is presumably a parody of Essex's façade to Emmanuel College at the end of the street.

Map 8

Ⓐ Fitzwilliam College chapel
Ⓑ Crystallographic Data Centre

Other buildings mentioned
① Christ's College
② Fitzwilliam College, original
    buildings
③ Downing College
④ Kettle's Yard

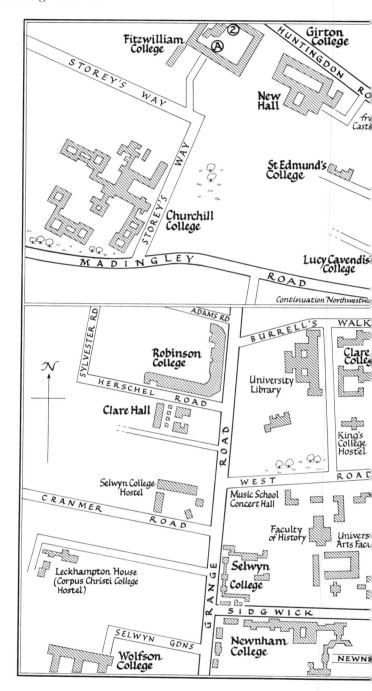

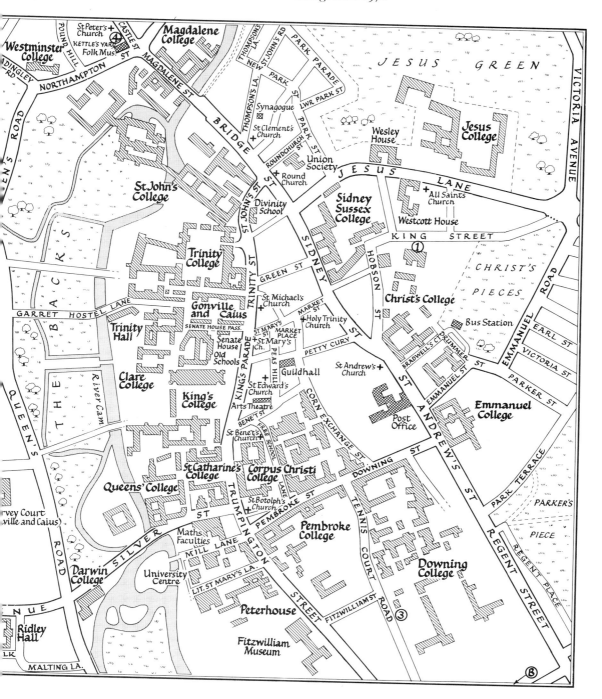

Many recent buildings in Cambridge as elsewhere in Britain have been in a 'neo-vernacular' style. Most are inoffensive but the least successful are rather clumsy. The best is represented by Kettle's Yard, a gallery constructed in 1970 as an extension to house the collection of Jim Ede, by Leslie Martin with David Owers. Externally clad in local stock brick and stained timber, it has a subtly lit and calm interior.

FITZWILLIAM COLLEGE CHAPEL

Fitzwilliam was one of the new post-war colleges although it had began as an 'approved society' in 1889, occupying Fitzwilliam House opposite the Museum in Trumpington Street. Denys Lasdun was the architect for the first new buildings, from 1958. Lasdun was later to be the architect of the National Theatre in London, and in Cambridge of an overscaled building for Christ's with a stepped section like Harvey Court's that has been subsequently re-faced on the King Street side. A more successful building was the Royal College of Physicians in Regent's Park, London, a headquarters that obeys all the rules of the Corbusian prescription yet is quite at home among the terraces of Nash. At Fitzwilliam he was faced with the problem of a low budget (it was one of the few Cambridge buildings to be constructed within the University Grants Commission's limits without additional funding) and the incorporation of an early nineteenth-century house, The Grove, in a plan which was designed to expand in several phases. The common rooms (hall, library and offices) are placed in a central block, with a vaulted concrete roof to the hall. The undergraduate staircases, which have random vertical window slits between expressed horizontal floor slabs, surround this block. In 1990 Richard MacCormac, of MacCormac Jamieson and Prichard, was employed to provide more undergraduate accommodation to the south, and in his more generously funded building he manages to be respectful to Lasdun while inventing a new variation of the Cambridge staircase which places straight-flight top-lit stairs transversely in a narrow block so that they interconnect on the top floor. This permits alternative escape routes in case of fire, something which traditional stair arrangements fail to do. In 1973 MacCormac had submitted an unsuccessful entry for the competition for Robinson College, with pavilion-like buildings reminiscent of Frank Lloyd Wright. At Fitzwilliam the references, in his handling of the wall-plane and use of internal top-lighting and mirrors, include the nineteenth-century architect, Sir John Soane, and for the chapel he retained an external appearance in harmony with Lasdun's work, while drawing on a rich history of architectural precedent.

The chapel sits at the end of one of Lasdun's ranges but is approached from beneath an external archway. The chapel proper occupies the equivalent of the first and second floors of the residential blocks, sitting over a ground-floor crypt. A pair of staircases curve around the crypt to emerge close to the altar, which is set against a large window looking at a tree in the garden of The Grove (Fig. 30). Formally, there is a play between

30 Fitzwilliam College Chapel

the square aedicule formed by the four pairs of concrete posts and the bulging brick shape of the chapel building. Daylight drops in the inter-space between. Iconographically, as the architect has explained, the chapel is treated as a 'vessel'. A ship has long been a symbol of the church itself and the word 'nave' may derive from the Latin 'navis', but MacCormac appeals also to the imagery of the sea in the writings of Carl Jung, and makes the reference explicit in the curved timber cladding to the soffit of the entrance arch. A comparison with chapels in two other post-war colleges, Churchill and Robinson, may be instructive. At Churchill a similarly controlled geometrical scheme was used but with gloomy non-reflective fair-faced brick walls. Robinson is similarly dark-toned, but is an unusual lozenge shape, with Piper's great glass window perversely but dramatically concealed from the congregation. By contrast, Fitzwilliam appears puritanical and lucid; its luminous space is one of the most successful twentieth-century interiors in Cambridge and lives up to the standards of the traditions it has inherited.

CAMBRIDGE CRYSTALLOGRAPHIC DATA CENTRE

The Cambridge Crystallographic Data Centre (CCDC) was established at the University of Cambridge Chemistry Laboratories in 1965. It compiles a computerised database containing comprehensive data for organic and organo-metallic compounds, studied by X-ray and neutron diffraction methods. The major applications are in pharmacology and chemistry, and the database is distributed to around 100 companies in Europe, Japan and the USA. It is these companies which provide the primary financial support to CCDC, which since 1989 has been incorporated as an independent non-profit institution with charitable status. It is administered by a Board, and the Director, Dr Kennard, was instrumental in appointing the Danish architect Erik Christian Sørensen for their new building. He had designed an excellent house for her in Cambridge thirty years before.

The CCDC building is situated within an area known as Newtown, an early nineteenth-century extension south of the city. In the 1960s a comprehensive redevelopment of the area was begun, with blocks of flats set in large areas of green space replacing the terraces. Only one pair of these blocks was built, immediately to the south of the CCDC site, before architectural sensibilities altered and the economics of housing provision changed. Its blank-walled, two-storey car park faces Union Road. A new school was built in the 1980s, set back from the street and looking like a Fenland bungalow. But the most disruptive intervention in the area was the University's own Chemistry Department on Lensfield Road, built on the site of William Wilkins' house for himself between 1953 and 1960. Though well-constructed and functional, it is an architecturally confused building. Its large areas of brickwork are punctuated by uncomfortably proportioned windows. Occasionally, and apparently at random, giant reconstructed-stone pilasters are introduced. The whole building sits as an overscaled object within its tarmac precinct because soon after its completion the University purchased and demolished the row of terrace houses on its southern fringe (where the CCDC now sits) to form a car park.

The way the CCDC building respects and interprets its awkward neighbours is one of its most impressive virtues. Sørensen saw the bungaloid school as the most inappropriate of the recent insertions and welcomed the challenge of making sense both of the stranded whale of the Chemistry building and the blank brick façade of the 1960s car park. Clasping the Chemistry building's south transept, the CCDC completely fills the space between the Chemistry building and Union Road. The building therefore has a south-facing front (Fig. 31), where the main entrance is, two sides, but no back.

Sectionally, it is arranged so that the principal workspaces are back-lit through a high south-facing clerestory on to the white-painted (and hence transformed) wall of the Chemistry building, with only small openings punched through the thick skin of the south wall. Inside, the building is ordered by serene static volumes rather than any exploitation of the dynamics of movement because utilitarian staircases are suppressed behind screen walls and only a silent glazed lift moves between floors and half-floors.

31 The Cambridge Crystallographic Data Centre

Sørensen took his patron, Olga Kennard, to King's College Chapel to persuade her that a large volume would suppress the effect of the furniture, and he was right: work stations for the research assistants disposed on the open floors hardly register in the space. Acoustically, however, the lofty room is not at all like King's Chapel because the ceilings, walls and floors are absorbent and the most insistent sound is the fountain on the first floor trickling into its crystal bath. Perhaps it is more like being in a huge hay-loft, where the darkness is enlivened by the occasional diagonal shaft of sunlight and where a soft footfall can hardly be heard.

The façade takes the ingredients used on the Chemistry building and transforms them. This is achieved partly through the superior quality of the materials, but mostly it is due to a surer eye: the infallible placing of voids in relation to solids. The architect succeeds in avoiding the arbitrariness of the weaker buildings of the 1950s by limiting his palette of materials so that every move in the plane of the wall tells. The effect is not to demean the adjoining Chemistry building because there is no knowing game or parody as one might expect some architects to attempt. The CCDC building makes such procedures look trivial yet it is difficult to extract a principle from the course that the architect has adopted. Sørensen's abstracted contextualism would hardly be a recipe for the average architect with a less sure eye and even in this instance leads to a building which may seem unfriendly to the layperson in its severity.

Internally a fastidious concern for detail is evident. The outside walls are clad entirely with perforated acoustic bricks, made in Flemsborg, of a delicate purple/pink. The painted brick screen walls to the four partitioned rooms have an exquisite profile on plan (accommodating a ventilation extract) which implies a gentle deflection around 300 mm diameter columns and creates a recess for bookshelves internally. The columns themselves are painted dark blue with thin white stripes, running through two storeys in the case of those under the rooflight – no mean testament to the painter's art.

In one sense this building is unprecedented (there are no obvious models for charitable research institutes), but at another level it is steeped in history. Sørensen's severe brick walls remind one of Imperial Rome or of Albi Cathedral. His internal spaces speak of a whole history of architecture, whether 'Gothic' in their verticality or 'classical' in their attention to profile and detail. A building that refers to generalised precedents rather than to particular ones, or to well-established conventions, may be less easy to assimilate than MacCormac's chapel at Fitzwilliam, but in 1993 it was voted 'building of the year' by the *Sunday Times* and the Royal Fine Arts Commission; if enlightened patronage can be found, we may conclude, the art of architecture is alive and well in Cambridge.

Notes on further reading

Jim Ede wrote a book about his gallery and its architecture entitled *A Way of Life: Kettle's Yard*.

For a fuller description of MacCormac's Fitzwilliam accommodation block and the first of Quinlan Terry's buildings at Downing College see my article in *Cambridge Magazine*; the description of the CCDC building is a condensed version of my article in *The Architect's Journal* of 8 July 1992.

A more general discussion of recent architecture is contained in my contribution to a symposium on Postmodernism in *The Cambridge Review* (vol. 110).

Glossary

abacus	The flat top above a capital, beneath the entablature
abbot	The head of a monastery
aedicule	Literally a little house; hence a house-like space framed by columns
aisle	Passage parallel to the nave of a church, separated from it by columns or piers
apse	Semicircular or polygonal projection, usually from the chancel of a church
arcade	A number of free-standing arches carried on columns or piers
Arts and Crafts	A term used to describe the architecture inspired by William Morris and his contemporaries relying on craftsmanship for this effect
atrium	Central court of a Roman house; recently a glazed-in court
attic	The space within the sloping roof of a building; or the wall in a building above the level of the entablature
baldacchino	A canopy, fixed or sometimes portable, suspended or carried on columns
balustrade	Dwarf wall supported on a series of small pillars
Baroque	The name given to seventeenth- and early eighteenth-century classical architecture, usually massive but spatially complex and theatrical in character.
barrel vault	The simplest form of vault, like a tunnel
battlement	A crenellated parapet; a low wall at the edge of a roof with alternating high and low portions as in a castle
bay window	An angled or curved projection containing windows
belfry	Upper storey in a church where bells are hung
boss	The ornamented knob at the junction of the ribs of a vault
brutalist	A term used by critics to describe 1950s Modernist buildings which employ 'béton brut' (rough concrete) and demonstrate the texture of the materials of which they are made
buttress	A projecting mass of masonry to provide additional strength to a wall; later Gothic architecture employs flying buttresses, which are in the form of a half-arch

Glossary

cantilever	Self-supporting projection
capital	The top of a column, usually decorated and in classical architecture within a recognised pattern
casement	A sidewards opening window, as opposed to a sash window which slides vertically
chancel	The east end of a church, containing the altar
chapter house	The room where the monks or nuns in a monastery or convent would assemble for meetings
cloister	An open roofed passage, often vaulted; in monasteries cloisters connect the church to the rest of the buildings
clunch	Porous chalky stone
combination room	A room where fellows of a college meet socially
cornice	The topmost projecting part of an entablature
crenellation	Alternating higher and lower portions of a parapet
crypt	Below-ground room in a church, originally used for burials
dado	The lower part of an interior wall, often panelled
Elizabethan	Style of architecture in England during the reign of Queen Elizabeth I (1558–1603)
entablature	The upper part of a classical order, consisting, from bottom to top, of architrave, frieze and cornice
façade	Literally face; the principal exterior wall face of a building
fan vault	A vault where the ribs spread out in a cone shape, resembling an open fan
flying buttress	See buttress
font	Bowl used to hold water for baptism
frieze	Central part of an entablature, decorated according to which order is employed; also used for any horizontal decorated band
gallery	The upper floor, above an aisle in a church and open to the nave
gargoyle	Water spout projecting from a roof, often carved to represent animals or human faces
hammer-beam	The wooden projection from a wall carrying arched braces or struts to form a roof support
Jacobean	Style of architecture in England during the reign of James I (1603–25)
keystone	The central stone of an arch, window head or vault
lancet	A tall slender window with a single pointed arch
lantern	A small turret with windows all around
light	(Single or double) window opening between mullions
lunette	Semicircular opening.
Mannerism	The name given to the style of classical architecture in Italy in the late sixteenth century, often contradictory, perverse or over-sophisticated in character
minstrels' gallery	Upper floor overlooking a larger room from which choirs or musicians would perform
mullion	The vertical post or division in a window dividing it into a number of lights

Glossary

nave	The central part of a church, west of the chancel since the altar is normally to the east
neo-Gothic	A revived Gothic style, originating in garden buildings in the mid-eighteenth century and widespread in the nineteenth century
newel	Solid central post holding up staircase and carrying the handrail or balustrade
oriel	A bay window, often on an upper floor but also used for large bays in college dining hall
parapet	Low wall at the edge of a roof or balcony
pediment	A triangular or segmentally curved panel at the gable of a building or over a door or window
Perpendicular	The final phase of English Gothic architecture, with repetitive vertical and horizontal subdivisions to windows or panels
pier	A solid masonry support either set against a wall or free-standing
pilaster	A shallow pier, or rectangular column in flattened shape, projecting slightly from the face of a wall
pinnacle	A little turret at the top of a spire or buttress
portcullis	Heavy timber or iron gate at the entrance to a castle
Purbeck marble	Exceptionally hard limestone, usually polished, from the Isle of Purbeck in Dorset
quadripartite	Divided into four parts
relieving arch	An arch set in a solid wall of masonry to assist in carrying the structural loads sideways above an opening
Renaissance	Term used to describe the architecture in Italy between about 1420 and 1550, referring to the rebirth of culture from a study of classical civilisation
render	Lime-based or cement-based mixture used to cover a wall surface
reveal	The edge of a window or door
rib vault	Vault with diagonal stone moulding
rustication	Wall made to look as if it is made from solid rocks
sash window	Vertically sliding window
segmented arch	An arch made up of curves or segments rather than a single semicircle
spandrel	Triangular piece at the side of an arch or between adjoining arches
springing	The point from which an arch or vault rises
string course	A continuous projecting horizontal band of masonry
stylobate	Continuous platform on which a row of columns rests
transept	The arms of a cross-shaped church, usually facing north and south, and meeting the nave at the crossing
triumphal arch	An archway erected by Roman emperors to celebrate their victories usually with a wide opening between two narrow ones
truss	Several timbers jointed together to act as a support for secondary beams
vault	An arched ceiling usually made in brick or stone, the simplest form being a barrel vault, like a tunnel

Bibliography

Appleyard, Brian, *The Pleasures of Peace: Art and Imagination in Post-War Britain*, London, Faber and Faber, 1989

Arnell, P. and Bickford, T., *James Stirling Buildings and Projects*, London, The Architectural Press, 1984

Atkinson, Thomas Dinham, *Cambridge Described and Illustrated, being a Short History of the Town and University*, London, Macmillan, and Cambridge, Macmillan and Bowes, 1897

Bury, Patrick, *A Short History of the College of Corpus Christi and the Blessed Virgin Mary*, Cambridge, Corpus Christi, 1949

Bury, Patrick, *The College of Corpus Christi and the Blessed Virgin Mary: A History from 1822–1952*, Cambridge, Corpus Christi, 1952

Clark, John Willis, *A Concise Guide to the Town and University of Cambridge, in an Introduction and Four Walks*, ninth revised edition, Cambridge, Bowes and Bowes, 1929

Clark, Kenneth, *The Gothic Revival: An Essay in the History of Taste*, third edition, London, John Murray, 1974

Clarke, Basil F. L., *Church Builders of the Nineteenth Century: A Study of the Gothic Revival in England*, London, Society for the Promotion of Christian Knowledge, 1938

Clifton-Taylor, Alec, *The Cathedrals of England*, London, Thames and Hudson, 1967

Collymore, Peter, *The Architecture of Ralph Erskine*, London, Granada Publishing, 1982

Crook, Alec C., *Penrose to Cripps: A Century of Building in the College of St John the Evangelist, Cambridge*, Cambridge University Press, 1978

Crook, Alec C., *From the Foundation to Gilbert Scott: A History of the Buildings of St John's College Cambridge 1511 to 1885*, Cambridge University Press, 1980

Crook, J. Mordaunt, *The Dilemma of Style: Architectural Ideas from the Picturesque to the Post-Modern*, London, John Murray, 1987

Cruickshank, Dan and Wyld, Peter, *London: The Art of Georgian Building*, London, The Architectural Press, 1975

Cunningham, Colin and Waterhouse, Prudence, *Alfred Waterhouse 1830–1905: Biography of a Practice*, Oxford University Press, 1992

Curtis, William, *Modern Architecture since 1900*, Oxford, Phaidon Press, 1982

Bibliography

Ede, Jim, *A Way of Life: Kettle's Yard*, Cambridge University Press, 1984

Fyfe, Theodore, *Architecture in Cambridge*, Cambridge University Press, 1942

Girouard, Mark, *Sweetness and Light: The Queen Anne Movement 1860–1900*, Oxford University Press, 1977

Grant, Michael, *Cambridge*, second edition, Oxford, Mowbray, 1976

Gray, Arthur, *The Town of Cambridge: A History*, Cambridge, W. Heffer and Son's Limited, 1925

Gray, Arthur and Brittain, Frederick, *A History of Jesus College, Cambridge*, revised edition, London, Heinemann, 1979

Haigh, Diane, 'M. H. Baillie Scott: 48 Storey's Way, Cambridge', *The Architect's Journal* 196, 22 July 1992

Hall, C. and Lovatt, R., 'The Site and Foundation of Peterhouse', *Proceedings of the Cambridge Antiquarian Society* 78 for 1989, Cambridge, 1990

Humphrey, S. C., *The Victorian Rebuilding of All Saints' Church Cambridge, or The Salt of Noble Sentiment in Jesus Lane*, London, The Ecclesiological Society, 1983

Jackson, Thomas Graham, *Recollections of Thomas Graham Jackson*, arranged and edited by Basil H. Jackson, Oxford University Press, 1950

Keynes, F. A., *By-ways of Cambridge History*, Cambridge University Press, 1947

Kidson, Peter, Murray, Peter and Thompson, Paul, *A History of English Architecture*, second edition, Harmondsworth, Penguin Books, 1979

Kornwolf, J. D., *M. H. Baillie Scott and the Arts and Crafts Movement*, London, Johns Hopkins University Press, 1972.

Kuhn, Thomas, *The Structure of Scientific Revolutions*, second edition, Chicago, University of Chicago Press, 1970

Laslett, Peter, *The World We Have Lost*, London, Methuen, 1965, third edition, Cambridge University Press, 1983

Liscombe, R. W., *William Wilkins 1778–1839*, Cambridge University Press, 1980

Louw, H. J., 'The Origin of the Sash Window', *Architectural History* 26, 1983, pp. 49–72

Lowenthal, David, *The Past is a Foreign Country*, Cambridge University Press, 1985

McKean, Charles, *Architectural Guide to Cambridge and East Anglia since 1920*, London, RIBA Publications Ltd, 1982

Maltby, Sally, MacDonald, Sally and Cunningham, Colin, *Alfred Waterhouse 1830–1905*, booklet to accompany RIBA Heinz Gallery Exhibition, London, 1983

Martin, J. L., *Buildings and Ideas 1933–1983*, Cambridge University Press, 1983

Martin, Leslie and March, Lionel, *Urban Space and Structures*, Cambridge University Press, 1972

Morgan, Iris and Gerda, *The Stones and Story of Jesus Chapel, Cambridge*, Cambridge, Bowes and Bowes, 1914

Muthesius, Stefan, *The High Victorian Movement in Architecture 1850–1870*, London, Routledge and Kegan Paul, 1972

Pevsner, Nikolaus, *Cambridgeshire*, in the series The Buildings of England, second edition, Harmondsworth, Penguin Books, 1970

Pevsner, Nikolaus, *Some Architectural Writers of the Nineteenth Century*, Oxford, Clarendon Press, 1972

Plommer, Hugh, *The Line of Duty*, Cambridge, published by the author, 1982

Purcell, Donovan, *Cambridge Stone*, London, Faber and Faber, 1967

Rackham, O., 'The Making of the Old Court', *Letter of the Corpus Association* 66, Michaelmas 1987 and 67, Michaelmas 1988

Raverat, Gwen, *Period Piece: A Cambridge Childhood*, London, Faber and Faber, 1952

Rawle, Tim, *Cambridge Architecture*, London, Trefoil Books, 1985

Ray, Nicholas, 'Cambridge Buildings in Context', *Cambridge Magazine* 23, 1988, pp. 278–83

Ray, Nicholas, 'Crystal Clear in Cambridge', *The Architect's Journal* 196, 8 July 1992, pp. 24–34

Ray, Nicholas, 'Postmodernism in Architecture', *The Cambridge Review* 110, no. 2305, 1989, pp. 53–66

Roberts, David, *The Town of Cambridge as it ought to be Reformed: the Plan of Nicholas Hawksmoor interpreted in an Essay by David Roberts*, Cambridge University Press, 1955

Robinson, Duncan and Wildman, Stephen, *Morris and Company in Cambridge*, catalogue of an exhibition at the Fitzwilliam Museum, Cambridge, Cambridge University Press, 1980

Robson, R., *Trinity College*, Norwich, Jarrold and Son, 1967

Rowe, Colin, 'The Blenheim of the Welfare State', *The Cambridge Review*, 31 October 1959, pp. 89–93

Royal Commission on Historical Monuments, *An Inventory of the Historical Monuments in the City of Cambridge*, in two parts, London, HMSO, 1959

Ruskin, John, *The Stones of Venice*, illustrated edition, London, G. Allen, 1905

Rutter, Frank, *Illustrated Guide to Cambridge*, Cambridge, W. Heffer and Sons, 1925

Saint, Andrew, *The Image of the Architect*, New Haven and London, Yale University Press, 1983

Salzman, L. F. (ed.), *The Victoria History of the County of Cambridge and the Isle of Ely*, London, Oxford University Press, 1948

Scott, M. H. Baillie, *Houses and Gardens*, London, 1906

Scott, M. H. Baillie and Beresford, A. E., *Houses and Gardens*, second revised edition, London, Architecture Illustrated, 1933

Sharp, Thomas, *Dreaming Spires and Teeming Towers: The Character of Cambridge*, Liverpool University Press, 1963

Sicca, Cinza Maria, *Committed to Classicism: The Building of Downing College, Cambridge*, Cambridge, Downing College, 1987

Stamp, G., 'Sir Giles Gilbert Scott', *Sir Giles Gilbert Scott and the Scott Dynasty*, ed. R. Dixon, London, South Bank Architectural Papers, 1980

Stokes, Adrian, *The Stones of Rimini*, London, Faber and Faber, 1934

Summerson, John, *Heavenly Mansions and Other Essays on Architecture*, London, Crescent Press, 1949

Summerson, John, *Architecture in Britain 1530 to 1830*, fourth edition, Harmondsworth, Penguin Books, 1963

Summerson, John, *The Classical Language of Architecture*, BBC booklet, introduction and accompaniment to six broadcast talks, London, BBC Publications, 1963, revised and enlarged edition, London, Thames and Hudson, 1980

Summerson, John, *The Unromantic Castle and Other Essays*, London, Thames and Hudson, 1990

Taylor, Kevin, *Central Cambridge: A Guide to the University and Colleges*, Cambridge University Press, 1994

Bibliography

Taylor, Nicholas, *Cambridge New Architecture*, second edition, Cambridge, privately published, 1965

Trachtenberg, Marvin and Hyman, Isabelle, *Architecture from Pre-History to Post-Modernism*, London, Academy Editions, 1986

Trevelyan, G. M., *Trinity College: An historical sketch*, Cambridge, Trinity College, 1943 and 1983

Twigg, J., *A History of Queens' College, Cambridge, 1448–1986*, Woodbridge, Boydell Press, 1987

Tzonis, Alexander and Lefaivre, Liane, *Classical Architecture: The Poetics of Order*, London and Cambridge, MA, MIT Press, 1986

Urry, John, *The Tourist Gaze: Leisure and Travel in Contemporary Societies*, London, Sage Publications, 1990

Watkin, David, *Thomas Hope and the Neo-Classical Idea*, London, John Murray, 1968

Watkin, David, *The Life and Work of C. R. Cockerell*, London, A. Zwemmer Limited, 1974

Watkin, David, *Morality and Architecture: The Development of a Theme in Architectural History and Theory from the Gothic Revival to the Modern Movement*, Oxford, Clarendon Press, 1977

Watkin, David, *The Triumph of the Classical: Cambridge Architecture 1804–1834*, Cambridge University Press for the Fitzwilliam Museum, 1977

Watkin, David, *The Architecture of Basil Champneys*, Cambridge, Newnham College, 1989

Whinney, Margaret, *Wren*, London, Thames and Hudson, 1971

White, James F., *The Cambridge Movement: The Ecclesiologists and the Gothic Revival*, Cambridge University Press, 1962

Willis, Robert and Willis Clark, John, *The Architectural History of the University of Cambridge and the Colleges of Cambridge and Eton*, 3 volumes, Cambridge University Press, 1886; reprinted with an introduction by David Watkin, 1988

Wollheim, Richard (ed.), *The Image in Form: Selected Writings of Adrian Stokes*, Harmondsworth, Penguin Books, 1972

Wren, Christopher, Jun., *Life and Works of Sir Christopher Wren, from The Parentalia or Memoirs by his son, Christopher*, Campden, Essex House Press, 1903

Wren Society, *Catalogue of Sir Christopher Wren's Drawings*, 20 volumes, Oxford University Press, 1924–43

Index of buildings and people

This index is confined to buildings, architects and critics. A **bold** number indicates a main entry; an *italicised* number indicates an illustration.

Aalto, Alvar, 32, 108, 111, 112
Adam, Robert, 69, 79
Alberti, L. B., 32, 37, 55, 78
All Saints, Jesus Lane, 30, 34, **82–5**, *84*
All Saints, Trinity Street, 30, 82
Aristotle, 37
Asplund, E. G., 96

Backs, The, **2–3**, 60, 72
Baker, Herbert, 76, 90, 117
Barnwell Priory, 10, 24
Basevi, George, 72
Bauhaus, 87, 104
Bernini, 58, 78
Bicknell, Peter, 104
Bodley, George F., 28, 30, **83–5**, 91, 93
Borromini, 78
Bridgeman, C., 3
Brown, 'Capability', 3
Burne-Jones, E., 34
Burrough, James, 58, 63
Butterfield, William, 83, 86, 90

Caius, Dr, 21, 26, 45, 55
Cam, River, 6
Castle Hill, 6, 10
CCDC, **121–4**, *123*
Champneys, Basil, 87, **90–2**
Charlemagne, 7, 12
Christ's College: Chancellor's Building, 104; King Street, 112; Fellows' Building, **48–51**, *49*, 52, 55, 117
Churchill College, **105**, 114, 121
CIAM, 105, 114

Clare College, 49, **51–2**, *53*; Chapel, 51, **58**, 96; Master's Lodge, 68; Memorial Court, 95–6
Clare Hall, 95, 106, **113–15**, *115*
Corpus Christi College: foundation, 25; Old Court, 25–6, *27*; Leckhampton House, 97

Devey, George, 83
Downing College, **75–7**, *77*, 117
Dowson, Philip, 95, 96–7
Durham, 10

Ely Cathedral: nave, 10; Lady Chapel, 24
Emmanuel College: Chapel, 50, 55; First Court, **58**, 117
Erskine, Ralph, 113–114
Essex, James, 30, 32, 33, **58**, 60, 66, 75, 117

Fitzwilliam College, 112, 120; Chapel, 120–1, *121*
Fitzwilliam Museum, 72–3
Fry, Maxwell, 104

Gibbons, Grinling, 62
Gibbs, James, 3, 20, 50, 59, 62, **65–6**, 79, 80
Girton College, 90
Gonville and Caius College: Caius Court, 45; Gate of Honour, 45–8, *46*; Tree Court, 45, **81**; Harvey Court, **106–8**, *107*, 120
Grey, Arthur, 7
Gropius, Walter, 104
Grumbold, Robert, 52
Grumbold, Thomas, 49, 52

Hawksmoor, Nicholas, 58, 62, **64–6**, 78, 79
History Faculty, 108–11, *109*

Hodgkinson, Patrick, 106
Holy Sepulchre, **12–14**, *15*, 74
Hope, Thomas, 75–7
Howell, W. G., 77, 105
Hughes, H. C., 104

Impington Village College, 104

Jackson, Thomas G., 42, 91, **92–4**, 117
Jesus College, 10, **33–4**, *35*; new library, 29
Jones, Inigo, **42**, 49, 94

Kahn, Louis, 113
Kennard, Olga, 122, 123
Kettles Yard, 120
King's College: Chapel, **43**, 73, 123; chancel stalls,
    screen, 43–5, *44*; Fellows' Building, 3, **64–6**, *65*;
    Market Hill, 107
King's Hall, 30
King's Parade, 4

Langley, Batty, 69
Lasdun, Denys, 112, **120**
Law School, **92–5**, *93*, 117
Le Corbusier, 64, **101**, 104, 111
Lethaby, W. R., 50
'Little Trinity', 59
Lloyds Bank, 82
Lucy Cavendish College, 87
Lutyens, Edwin, 84, **87–8**, 98, 117

MacCormac, Richard, **120–1**, 124
Mackintosh, C. R., 98
Macmillan and Metzstein, 105
Magdalene College: Benson Court, 87, 90; Pepys
    Library, **42**, 50
Malcolm Street, 59
Martin, J. Leslie, **106–8**, 111, 112, 120
Michaelhouse, 25, 30
Michelangelo, 30, 42, 49, 50, 60
Miller, Sanderson, 69
Mond Laboratory, 104
Morris, William, 28, 34, 74, 82, 87
Muthesius, Hermann, **87**, 97

Nevile, Thomas, **30**, 31, 60
Newnham College, 87, **90–2**, *91*

Owers, David, 120
Oxford, 17, 21, 58, 59; Brasenose College, 112;
    Examination Schools, 93; Manor Road libraries,
    111; Mansfield College, 92; Merton College, 11,
    17, 92; New College, 29, 92

Palladio, Andrea, 42, 58, 60, 78
Park Terrace, 59
Pater, Walter, 86

Paxton, Joseph, 87
Pembroke College: Chapel, 42, 55; Red Building,
    81–2, *81*
Peterhouse, 17, 21, 36, 58; Chapel, 24, **42**, 50; Fen
    Court, 104; Master's Lodge, 59, **66–8**, *67*, 82
Pevsner, Nikolaus, 5, 25, 68
Powell and Moya, 111–13
Prior, E. S., 92, **94–5**, 114
Pugin, A. W. N., 34, **73**, 83, 105

Queens' College: Cloister Court, 29, 30; Cripps
    Court, 111; foundation, 27; plan, 21, **22–3**, 27,
    28

Rackham, Oliver, 25
Raverat, Gwen, 87
Rawle, Tim, 5, 10
Richardson, Albert, 104
Rickman, Thomas, 3, 24, **72**, 73, 78, 112
Roberts, David, 68, 87, 109
Robinson College, **105**, 121
Rogers, Richard, 113
Round Church, **12–14**, *15*, 74
Rowe, Colin, 105
Royal Institute of British Architects, 91
Ruskin, John, 66, **83**, 86

Salvin, Anthony, 12, 32, 74
San Vitale, Ravenna, 82
Scott, George Gilbert, 10, 81, 86, 92
Scott, Giles Gilbert, 3, 83, **95–6**
Scott, M. H. Baillie, 97–9
Scott, Walter, 69
Senate House, 20, 66
Serlio, Sebastiano, **40**, 42, 47, 48, 49, 55, 58
Shaw, R. Norman, 84, 86–7, 91
Sheppard, Richard, 105
Smithson, Alison and Peter, 105
Smythson, Robert, 49
Soane, John, 120
Sørensen, Erik Christian, 122–4
SPAB, **74**, 82
St Andrew the Less, 24
St Bene't's, 7, 11, **12–14**, *13*, 25, 26
St Catharine's College, 62–4, *63*
St Clement's, 7, 24
St Edward's, 24
St John's College: 1712 bridge, 52; New Court, 3,
    72; playing fields, 6, 7; School of Pythagoras, **11**,
    112; Cripps Building, 111–13, *113*
St Mary's (Little), 17, 24
St Mary's (The Great), 20, 25, 33
St Michael's, 25
St Paul's, 73
St Peter's, *frontispiece*, 14–16, *16*
Stevenson, J. J., 50–1, 87, 91, 92
Stirling, James, 105, **108–11**

Stokes, Adrian, 108
Storey's Way, No. 48, 97–9, *99*
Street, G. E., 83, 86
Summerson, John, 53, 54

Team X, 113
Terry, Quinlan, 77, 117
Trinity College: foundation, 3; fountain, *31*, 45;
    Great Court, 30–2, *31*, 58; Hall screen, 45;
    Library, 3, 29, 54, 55, **60–2**, *61*; stair; Master's
    Lodge, 68

University, foundation, 17
University Library: New, 3, 20, **95–7**, *97*, 110; Old,
    69, **78–80**, *79*, 110

Vanbrugh, John, 64, 78
Vitruvius, 37, 40

Voysey, C. F. A., 98

Waterhouse, Alfred, 45, **80–2**, 83, 86, 90
Watkin, David, 80, 85, 99, 116
Webb, Philip, 86, 104
Werkbund, 87, 104
Wilkins, William, 4, 25, 26, 64, 66, **69–72**, **75–7**,
    78, 92
Willis, R. and Clark, J. R. W., 5, 20, 48, 58, 64
Wilson, Colin St. J., 106
Wimpole Hall, 59, 69
Wordsworth, William, 32
Wren, Christopher, 3, 29, 32, 42, 52, **54–8**, **60–2**,
    64, 73, 78, 79, 117
Wren, Matthew, 55
Wright, Frank Lloyd, 120
Wright, Stephen, 66, 79
Wyatt, James, 72, 75–6